KING OF THE COWBOYS

TY MURRAY

with

STEVE EUBANKS

KING

of the

COWBOYS

ATRIA BOOKS

New York   London   Toronto   Sydney   Singapore

ATRIA BOOKS
1230 Avenue of the Americas
New York, NY 10020

ISBN: 0-7434-6371-4

First Atria Books hardcover edition May 2003

10 9 8 7 6 5 4 3 2 1

ATRIA BOOKS is a trademark of Simon & Schuster, Inc.

For information regarding special discounts for bulk purchases,
please contact Simon & Schuster Special Sales at 1-800-456-6798 or
business@simonandschuster.com

Manufactured in the United States of America

In memory of Dean "Doc" Pavillard, who was like a second father to me, and to Tres Hazelton, who was like a brother to me. I miss you both.

INTRODUCTION

Eight Seconds

IT COMES DOWN to this. All the work, all the dreams, all the sweat, tears, blood, mud, fear, doubt, sacrifices, and victories boil down to this one moment in this dirt-filled arena. Everything I've dreamed of, everything I've worked for my entire life, comes down to these final eight seconds, which is how long I hope to stay on the back of a 2,200-pound brindle called Hard Copy.

I don't know much about him, but I've never known much about the bulls I ride until I'm sitting on their back. In my mind, too much information about roughstock is counterproductive. Over the years I've seen bull riders study the tendencies of the animals they draw, but it can backfire. The minute you think you can outsmart a bull and anticipate what he's going to do is the minute you get driven into the ground like a dart. The best bulls in rodeo are unpredictable. Trying to outsmart them can lead cowboys to outsmart themselves.

The only things I know about Hard Copy are that he is owned by Harper and Morgan, that he isn't successfully ridden very often, and that he is enormous. This bull is so big his hindquarters won't fit in the seven-foot-long chute.

The gate men can't close the slide gate behind him, so they tie a rope behind his haunches. He doesn't put up too much of a fuss, but that's because nobody's sitting on his back yet. The fuss will come later. Hard Copy is a tough draw.

I know one more thing: Hard Copy is the only thing standing between me and a record-breaking seventh all-around cowboy world championship, a goal I've been working toward my whole life.

Most people aren't fortunate (or some would say cursed) enough to have their life's work come down to a single, defining moment. It's a rare occurrence when a lawyer, banker, artist, or minister can point to one moment and say, "That's the instant that defined everything I've worked for." A lot of people can look back and point to this moment or that as a time that changed their life, but to have your defining moment in front of you for all the world to see, and to know the importance of that moment ahead of time, is something few people experience. It's even rare among athletes. Every kid who's ever picked up a basketball dreams of sinking the game-winning three-pointer in the seventh game of the NBA Finals, but few of the greatest NBA players get that chance. Any kicker who straps on a pair of shoulder pads dreams of booting the last-second field goal to win the Super Bowl, but you can count the number who have actually done it on one hand. Junior golfers spend hours on the practice green telling themselves, "This putt is to win the U.S. Open," but not many will realize that dream.

I'm fortunate, not cursed. My moment is right in front of me.

Sitting in the locker room at the Thomas and Mack Center at UNLV, home of the Runnin' Rebels, I take a small wire brush and run it up and down that part of my bull rope that has turned gray from all the rosin I've applied throughout the year. I rub with just enough pressure to remove the excess rosin without fraying the rope, just as I've done thousands of times before. Then I crush a few rocks of rosin in the palm of my riding glove and rub it onto the top and the bottom of the worn leather-laced handle, as well as along that section of rope I know I will be holding when the gate opens and Hard Copy tries to throw me into the first row of seats. It's always the same routine, nothing fancy, nothing different. I've ridden plenty of tough bulls in my life. I won't let the importance of the situation force a change in my routine.

I take a couple of deep breaths as I work the rosin into the rope, careful as always not to get any of the sticky stuff on the wear strip. This is my seventh trip to the Professional Rodeo Cowboys Association (PRCA) national finals in Las Vegas. The previous times I've walked away with the all-around world championship buckle. I'm as comfortable in these surroundings as anyone could be, but this time things are different. Unlike other years, when I've walked away with the title by a mile, this one is close. Herbert Theriot, who competes in calf roping and bulldogging, is on a heck of a run. I don't know exactly where he stands—I never watch the points too closely, figuring that if I do my best on every ride, the scores will take care of themselves—but I know this is as close as any championship has been in a number of years. If I'm going to become the first cowboy in history to win seven all-around world titles, I have to bear down. I have to ride this bull.

Another breath, in through the nose, out through the mouth . . . *whew.* I lean down and tighten the straps of my bull riding spurs. Then I take out a roll of athletic tape and wrap a strip snuggly around my wrist. I rip off several small strips of tape with my teeth and run them between my fingers, covering the calluses that have replaced most of the skin on my right hand. Another strip around my wrist and more tape around my knuckles and I'm almost ready.

The crowd noise rumbles through the corridors. It's certainly louder than I remember from years past. Twenty thousand people can shake the rafters when they want to. Maybe it's the drama of the moment, the closeness of the competition, or that this is the tenth and final round of the biggest rodeo in the world.

I'm happy to have the crowd noise as a distraction. I can't think about the number of times I've dreamed of this moment. I can't let my mind wander to the thousands of rides I've made in preparation for this night, and I can't think about the endless hours I've spent on a mechanical bull in my parents' backyard envisioning this ride. I sure as hell can't let myself think back to Mrs. Simmons's fifth-grade class, even though I've been asked about it a zillion times throughout my career.

Mrs. Simmons, a nice lady who did her best to teach a bunch of rowdy ten-year-olds to think creatively and write coherently, had asked us all to write a paper answering the question: "If you could do anything in your life, what would it be?" Most of my classmates wrote lengthy papers on being astronauts, secret agents, doctors, lawyers, and firemen. My answer was short and to the point: "I want to beat Larry Mahan's record." Larry was the greatest rodeo cowboy in history, my idol, a man who had won six world all-around championships. Now, fifteen years after writing that one-line essay, I am gunning for a record-breaking seventh all-around title.

I have to stay focused. Bulls don't know jack about records, and they don't care. Hard Copy doesn't know me; he doesn't know the situation, and even if he did, it doesn't matter. All he wants to do is throw me off his back. All I need to do is stay on him for eight of the longest seconds in sports.

With my glove in my back pocket and the small leather thong I use to tie the glove in place draped around my neck, I walk out of the locker room, down the corridor where Jerry Tarkanian's Rebels made many a championship trip, and up the small stairway onto the platform behind the chutes. I am the last rider, so I still have a little time.

Hard Copy is already in the chute, or as close as he can get given his size. Anybody who has never been around the sport would think we have a rhinoceros in here. As always, I climb onto the slats and place the sole of my right boot on the bull's back just to let him know I'm here. Hard Copy snorts and bristles, which is what I expect. I slowly climb over so my feet are on each side of the three-and-a-half-foot-wide chute.

I'm always careful to keep my boots running straight down the slats so my spurs are pointing behind me, but I pay extra attention to my feet today. This bull takes up every inch of the chute, and I don't want my spurs accidentally grabbing him. I also don't want to injure myself before getting out of the chute. With my feet running parallel to the bull's body, I don't have to worry about him moving in the chute and tearing up my ankle.

Once in position, I slowly lower myself onto Hard Copy's back with my feet still on the slats. I keep my knees bent and back straight just in case Hard Copy objects to my presence and tries to throw me forward in the chute. Slowly and precisely, I drop the loop of my bull rope down the left side of the bull while Chad Klein, my good friend and traveling partner, grabs the loop with a hook and pulls it underneath Hard Copy's thick underside. When I can see that the rope isn't twisted, I grab the loop and pull the tail through it. Then I adjust the rope so the handle is topside and the two cowbells are dangling on the underside of the bull's big belly. Once the rope is in place, I tie it off and slowly stand. Hard Copy has cooperated so far.

I climb out of the chute and slowly roll my head from side to side to loosen the muscles in my neck and upper back while shaking my hands and arms to stay relaxed. Over the years

I've learned to control my nerves by never allowing myself to be distracted. It took a few years and a few bad rides when I was under pressure, but I finally realized that the only moment I control is the one happening right now. A second ago is gone forever, and a second from now I have no idea what's coming, so there is never a reason to get ahead of myself. Nervousness creates tension, which slows reaction times. That's why I've worked from an early age at staying in the moment, not letting anything distract me from the present.

Sure, I have butterflies. Everybody does. But I want to use the butterflies to my advantage; to focus on the bull and the ride, and to stay as relaxed as possible.

In a small area behind the chutes I bend over and grab my ankles, stretching my hamstrings one final time. Then I cross my legs and lean into a hip-flexor stretch. Finally, I spread my legs wide and shift my weight from side to side to stretch my groin, the same routine I've gone through my whole career. Stretching gets my blood flowing and keeps me calm.

"Two more riders," the chute boss shouts. We're down to the last three riders, two more, then me. It's time to get my motor running.

I put on my glove and tie it to my wrist with the leather thong that I've been carrying around my neck. I don't watch the riders ahead of me. When the bull just ahead of me leaves the chute, I climb back into my chute and put my boot back on Hard Copy's back, another reminder that I'm still around. I sit on him with my feet on the slats, just as I did a few moments before. Then I hand the tail of my rope to Chad so I can adjust my handle, centering it right behind Hard Copy's shoulder blades. I check the position of the bells. Only a few seconds left. This is it.

At this point a wave of calm passes over me. I've gone through this routine tens of thousands of times in my life and millions of times in my mind. Now it's time to do what I know best.

I place my gloved right hand in the handle so my pinky is running down Hard Copy's spine, just where I want it. Then Chad pulls my rope tight. I take the rope, wrap it into my gloved hand, and slide my crotch forward until I'm almost sitting on my hand. With everything in place, I take one last deep breath and nod.

Bulls can come out of the chute a hundred different ways, so I always try to remain as upright and neutral as possible in that first critical second. This is no exception. When Hard Copy commits out of the gate, I take hold with my spurs.

He leaps forward and up with the force of a small explosion, thrusting his back legs up and out. He's "droppy," a bull that kicks while his front feet are still off the ground. I counter by adjusting my free arm, leaning forward, then quickly leaning back as the bull dips and noses in an attempt to throw me.

Two seconds.

Hard Copy's force and strength doesn't surprise me, but his agility when he changes directions is impressive for a bull this big. I sense him changing leads, which gives me a millisecond's advantage, just enough time to react.

Three seconds . . . four.

I'm as relaxed as I've ever been on an animal, reacting to each move as if we had choreographed this and practiced it ahead of time. Every move he makes, I make a perfect countermove. He spins left and I shift my center of gravity. He looks right and I adjust. You couldn't blow me off this bull with a cannon.

Five seconds.

The crowd is screaming, but I don't hear anything, not the sound of my own breath, and not the thuds every time Hard Copy hits the ground. All I'm waiting on is the horn at the end of my eight seconds.

Six seconds . . . seven.

I keep my feet heavy and low on a bull with my weight centered in my thighs and groin. From this position I can stay in control.

In the final moments, Hard Copy leaps straight up and throws his head back in a last-ditch effort to shake me. But I'm on for the duration, and both of us know it.

Eight seconds!

The horn sounds like a thousand trumpets when it goes off. I've done it! I've hit the buzzer-beater, kicked the last-second field goal, drained the breaking twenty-footer for a birdie on the last hole, hit the game-winning grand slam. I've ridden the ride I needed. My lifelong dream has finally come true.

When Hard Copy pitches to the left, I reach down with my free hand, grab the end of my rope, pull my wrap, lean forward, and wait for him to peak. When his back legs kick, I release the rope with both hands as I let the bull's momentum throw me clear on his right side. I stick my landing, bending my knees to absorb the shock and crouching to insure that Hard Copy doesn't kick me as he passes.

In the next second, the sounds of the crowd return and I hear and see twenty thousand people standing and cheering. It's the greatest sound I've ever heard. While I'm not one for postride celebrations, I can't help standing in that arena a few extra seconds with my fists in the air.

Then I trot off toward the gate. A crowd of familiar faces waits to greet me outside the arena. At the front of the line, ahead of my friends, fellow riders, and the media, is a person I never expected to see, especially not on this night.

Larry Mahan extends his hand to me. "Congratulations, Ty," says the man whose record I've just broken. "I've known for a lot of years that this night was coming. I'm just glad I could be here to see it."

I'm glad too. It has been a long, tough road, sometimes tougher than I thought I could handle, but I've finally done it.

"I don't know what to say, Larry," I tell him. "Thanks for being here."

"I wouldn't have missed it for the world," he says.

That makes two of us.

KING OF THE COWBOYS

1

The Cowboy Way

"SO," HE SAID, "why do you do it?"

I've been giving interviews most of my life, so this one was nothing unusual. We were outside the locker room at a Professional Bull Riders (PBR) event sitting on a stack of portable seats, the kind you'd find on an arena floor during a concert. The reporter asked some intelligent questions—it's always nicer when these guys have done their homework—but after a few minutes he asked that question, the one I'd heard more than any other since I'd begun riding.

The people who ask that question are always sincere. After several thousand interviews I expect it. But I still have a hard time answering it, not because I don't know why I'm a cowboy, but because the concept of the cowboy way is so foreign to some people that I have a hard time boiling it down to a simple sound bite.

"I'm a cowboy because I've always been a cowboy," I said

to this reporter. It was the umpteenth time I'd used that line, but I wasn't sure my media buddies got it. "I was born to it."

The reporter's eyes glazed over, and I knew I needed to do a better job of explaining myself. As far as I was concerned, asking a cowboy why he's a cowboy is like asking a Frenchman why he's French. Still, I needed to give it another shot.

"A cowboy is a cowboy no matter how he makes his living," I said. "Not all of us wear chaps and hats. You'll find plenty of cowboys wearing Brooks Brothers' suits on Wall Street, or playing in the NFL. Those real estate developers who borrow millions to build big office towers, a lot of them are cowboys. The cowboy way is about how you approach things, whether you're talking about a businessman, an artist, or a housewife. Being a cowboy is in your DNA. You either have it or you don't."

I still wasn't sure I was getting through to this reporter, so I tried another tack. "Look. When I won my first all-around championship, I was twenty years old. Almost every reporter asked me if I was surprised by how well I'd done so early in my career. That seemed funny to me. They asked it as if I just woke up one morning and found a gold buckle on my belt. I'd been working to win that first all-around championship since I was two years old.

"Being a cowboy was never a conscious choice. I never considered doing anything in life other than rodeo.

"Why do I do it? From the time I was old enough to walk I've always known where I wanted to go with my life, and I grew up in an environment where if I worked my butt off every day, I knew I would get there.

"I do it because it's all I've ever wanted, and all I've ever known. Not a lot of people can say that."

MY COWBOY GENES run deep. Riding and ranching have been my family's trade for almost a century, and our history mirrors the history of rodeo itself. Near the turn of the millennium I was given the nickname "the king of the cowboys," but at the turn of the last century, members of my father's family were blazing trails that make my life look tame by comparison.

The Miller Brothers' 101 Ranch, which at its peak was the largest working ranch in America, encompassed 110,000 acres near the town of Ponca City in northern Oklahoma between Oklahoma City and Wichita, Kansas. According to one of the brochures the Millers printed in 1910, "The 101 Ranch is the wonderspot and showplace of all the great southwest. Here is ranching in all its old-time picturesqueness. Here are the thousands of cattle and horses, the unblocked trails and cattle pastures, the unchanged cowboys and the Wild West cowgirls, the round-up camps, the corrals, and many tribes of primitive Indians living undisturbed in wigwam, lodge, and rough house."

The Millers also raised buffalo, ostriches, camels, elephants, sea turtles, and poultry. They grew wheat, apples, peaches, grapes, cherries, corn, potatoes, and oats. The ranch had its own oil wells that pumped fuel to run its vehicles, which included its own fleet of trains with 150 freight cars and Pullmans. They had their own bank with their own 101 Ranch currency called Miller Script, which could be spent at a general store with a tame black bear chained to the hitching post out front. The store advertised everything "from a needle to a Ford," but the bear was particularly fond of soda pop. Miller Script became so popular that it was accepted within a hundred-mile radius of the ranch (and was not infrequently used to pay off gambling debts).

The spread was so large it had its own power plant, oil refinery, phone system, post office, school, tannery, ice plant, laundry, saloon, café, woodworking shop, packing plant, cannery, and dude ranch. It also had some of the greatest and some of the most notorious cowboys in history working as hands.

George Washington Miller (the founder of the 101 and father of the brothers George, Joe, and Zack) had been through his share of scuffs with the law, a tradition he passed on to his sons. Joe was a convicted felon, and all the brothers were linked at one time or another to questionable activities. It shouldn't have surprised anyone that the Millers didn't check the backgrounds of their hands. Some of the cooks, cowhands, wranglers, and roustabouts were thieves, rustlers, and cold-blooded killers. But the Millers never seemed to mind. As long as you were a tough cowboy willing to work, you were welcome at the 101.

Ranching was a profitable business, but the brothers saw other opportunities. With the invention of the automobile, the Wright brothers' breakthrough at Kitty Hawk, the completion of the cross-country railroad, and the industrial revolution in high gear, a lot of Americans longed for a reminder of the old West. The Millers happily obliged. With so many great frontiersmen working and living on the ranch, Joe, George, and Zack began producing the 101 Ranch Wild West Show, a riding, roping, steer-wrestling, and trick-shooting extravaganza. The show was a big hit. Teddy Roosevelt came to the 101 to see it. So did John D. Rockefeller, William Randolph Hearst, General John Pershing, and Admiral Richard Byrd, who toured the ranch on an elephant not long after returning from the north pole.

These famous visitors and thousands of others like them paid to see the cowboys at the 101 do what they'd been doing in their spare time for free. After a day of working cattle, groups of hands would gather by the Salt Fork River and entertain themselves by riding bulls and broncs and wrestling steers. One of the most famous of these cowboys, a black man named Bill Pickett, got so mad at an uncooperative steer one day he jumped off his horse and bit the steer on the nose, holding on with his teeth like a bulldog. From that day forward Bill Pickett was considered the father of bulldogging.

It seemed odd to the cowboys that folks would pay to see them ride, rope, and shoot, but they weren't complaining. Bill Pickett became a star showman, one of the main attractions. The show got so popular that the Millers took it on the road, traveling from New York to California with cowboys, Indians, cattle, and horses in tow. When Hollywood started producing moving pictures with cowboys and Indians, the 101 provided the talent.

Just before the Christmas of 1911 the citizens of Venice, California, woke up to a surprise when they looked out their windows. There, perched on Venice Pier, were one hundred Ponca Indians with their tepees. The Indians, along with seventy-five cowboys and twenty-five cowgirls, were in town to film a movie, even though none of the participants had ever seen a moving picture show. But the new actors didn't stay ignorant very long. Hollywood silent-movie stars such as Tom Mix, Buck Jones, Hoot Gibson, and William Eagleshirt got their start as hands on the 101, and as performers in the Wild West Show.

The movies netted the Millers a fortune, but it was the live performances that drew the biggest crowds. In a 1929 *Time* magazine article, the show the Millers had created was described as "the incarnation of that vanished West in which cowboys had not become associated with drugstores and Indians were not graduates of Carlisle. Begun informally, casually, when the Millers permitted some of their cowboys to perform at a local fair, the 101 Ranch Show grew into a circus that netted the Millers a million dollars a year. Sideshows it had, and freaks, and many a Bearded Lady and Human Skeleton. But it was essentially a Wild West Show, with buffaloes and cattle, cowmen and cowgirls, pistols and scalping knives, and the sure-fire big scene of the Attack on the Stage Coach, with round-eyed, heart-pounding spectators writhing on the edges of pine-board seats." Little did the Millers know they had created what would become the modern rodeo, an American tradition that would outlast them all.

Buffalo Bill Cody rode in the 101 Show. So did a young Will Rogers, who did rope tricks on horseback. The U.S. army even allowed its most famous POW, the Apache chief Geronimo, to ride, shoot, and skin a buffalo in the 101 Show for the entertainment of the fans.

Among those who performed regularly were a group of cowboys known as the Schultz brothers. There were seven of them: Walter, Guy, Clarence, Troy, Will, Grover, and Floyd. Guy wrangled with Bill Pickett, rode broncs, and bulldogged buffalo. As part of the show he would jump from the running board of a Ford to bulldog a steer or a buffalo. He also rode the Hall of Fame bronc Midnight. Along with his brother Floyd, the two Schultzes were considered the best wild-horse racers and relay racers of their day. They were also great cowboys, something they never forgot even as they were traveling the countryside performing.

Guy was billed as a "champion bronc buster," and he toured Chicago, Detroit, New York, and Cleveland riding bareback and saddle broncs for folks who'd never seen a real cowboy. In the summer of 1915, Guy toured the country with boxing champion Jess "the Great White Hope" Willard, who had won the heavyweight title by knocking out Jack

Johnson in the twenty-sixth round of a fight in Havana, Cuba. Willard joined the show and was billed as "a cowboy from Kansas," even though he was a boxer first and a cowboy second.

Walter Schultz was a well-known mugger on the ranch. In those days there were no bucking chutes, so the mugger's job was to hold the bronc while the cowboy got on him. It was a tough job for a serious cowboy, and Walter fit that bill. While his brothers traveled, he stayed on the ranch, which suited him better. A young Potawatomi Indian girl had caught his eye, and Walter wasn't too interested in hitting the trail, even if it was for places like Chicago and Hollywood.

When the girl, named Josephine Papan, turned fourteen, Walter married her and moved her into his tent along the banks of the Salt Fork River. Life was hard, but simple. Walter continued to work as a mugger, while Josephine strung trotline across the river, sometimes catching catfish that weighed over a hundred pounds. She would string the fish up from a nearby tree and clean them like you would skin a buck. They bathed and drank from the river and cooked on an open fire. For the Schultzes, the Wild West wasn't something you had to see in a show. It was the way they lived every day. In time they had a daughter they named Georgia. And Georgia is my grandmother.

My great-grandfather and his brothers were the original rodeo cowboys before anyone knew what a rodeo was. By 1932, the Millers were mired in financial problems

brought on by the Great Depression. People were strug-
gling to feed their families. Entertainment luxuries like
Wild West shows were well down on most folk's priority list,
so the ranch was no longer profitable. That same year Bill
Pickett died of his injuries on the ranch when a bronc kicked
him in the head. Later, with the debts mounting and the
Depression raging, the great 101 Ranch went bankrupt.
Now all that's left are photos, a few scattered buildings,
Pickett's grave, and a cowboy legacy that has touched every
one of us.

Georgia Schultz, my grandmother, grew up and married Harold Murray, my grandpa. In 1941 they had a son
they named Butch. He is my dad.

DAD NEVER LIVED on the 101, or The One, as the
hands called it, but he grew up with the same cowboy values
that his grandpa and great-uncles had learned on the ranch.
When Dad was nine years old, his grandpa Walter and his
great-uncle Guy took him out on a broncy colt. As Dad was
getting the colt broke, a school bus full of football players
rode by. The kids, being too full of themselves for their own
good, started beating their hands on the side of the bus trying to spook the colt.

"Hey. You boys cut that out," Walter shouted.

All of a sudden the bus slid to a halt on the gravel road
and the football team came filing off. It seemed the coach

had told his team to go teach those two old men a lesson. They might have succeeded if it hadn't been for Walter's loyal old dog named Jim. According to my dad, "All he had to do was say, 'Get 'em, Jim,' and the dog would latch onto an arm and drag one of them off." The two aging, gray-haired ranch hands (with the help of Jim the dog) whipped an entire football team that afternoon. Nobody ever messed with the old men again.

Two years later at the ripe old age of eleven, Dad began work as Walter's free jockey, riding in match races in Oklahoma and Texas. Once again Walter was there, toughening him up every step of the way. "He had me riding racehorses without touching the reins," Dad said. "That'll sober you up pretty quick, especially when you're eleven years old and going thirty-five to forty miles an hour on a horse. But I figured the hurting I'd get from falling off was less than what I'd get from him if I touched those reins."

Dad's not a big man, but by the time he was a teenager he was too big to ride racehorses. That's when he started breaking colts for a living, honing the horseman skills he would use for the rest of his life. By the time he was twenty, Dad was breaking fifty horses a year, working all week in the breaking pen and riding in rodeos on the weekends. He loved to compete in rodeos, even though he spent all week breaking horses. Horses were his life, and his passion. He loved them more than anything, with one exception.

Three days after Joy Myers turned eighteen, Butch Murray married her. Mom knew what she was getting into when she married a cowboy. She was a two-time world champion girls bull rider in the Little Britches Rodeo. In fact, she won the National Little Britches all-around title thirty years to the day before I won it. She also came from a great rodeo family. Her brother, my uncle Butch Myers, was a world champion steer wrestler.

Mom and Dad moved to Arizona, where Dad gained a good reputation for being able to break the toughest colts. Owners would send colts in by the truckload, because they knew Dad was the best. He worked from dawn till dusk every day, always giving it everything he had. There was no other way, because if you weren't giving it your all in the breaking pen, you were crazy and soon to be laid up with an injury. This was not a job where you could ever mail it in. But it would never have occurred to Dad to give anything other than all he had, whether he was working in the breaking pen or rodeoing on the weekends. That right there was the cowboy way. It was a lesson he had learned by watching his grandpa and his great-uncles, and one I learned by watching him.

The family home in Glendale, Arizona, was a singlewide trailer with corrals, a breaking bin, and an arena out back. In the summer, Dad and Mom would move to an old adobe house on a ranch in Peña Blanca, New Mexico. Dad worked as race starter at The Downs at Santa Fe, Ruidoso Downs, The Downs at Albuquerque, and the Albuquerque State Fair.

Mom rode horses every day until 1962, when she discovered she was pregnant. My sister Kim was born that year, and a year later they had my other sister, Kerri.

I came along in October of 1969. If there were any doubts that I'd been born a cowboy, they were removed when my parents took me home from the hospital wearing a diaper, a T-shirt, a blanket, and a pair of cowboy boots. Two days out of the womb and I was ready to ride.

BECAUSE I ACHIEVED so much success at such an early age, questions have come up about my parents. Did they push me? Were they overbearing? When they realized I had a talent, did they turn into stage parents? The questions are natural given some of the horror stories I've read and heard about with other athletes in other sports. But in my case the questions are almost funny. My parents never pushed me toward rodeo a day in my life. They never had to. If anything, they had to make a conscious effort not to hold me back.

Before I was out of diapers, I was climbing on top of Mom's Singer sewing machine cover, the perfect mechanical bull for a thirteen-month-old. I'd grab the plastic handle with my right hand, palm up just as I'd seen Dad doing, then I'd raise my left arm high in the air and rock and spur that case until I wore it out. A few months later I progressed to the arm of the couch, a bigger (or at least taller) challenge. Mom swears that my first words were "I'm a bull rider."

When I could finally walk, I would chase my dog, Freckles, around the yard trying to rope her. And by the time I could talk, I was begging my parents to let me ride. It didn't hurt that I saw my dad breaking colts all day, every day, and that we spent our weekends at rodeos, but to say that my parents pushed me toward being a cowboy is a joke.

I once heard someone say to my mother, "Joy, when Ty was little, was he ever scared to get on a calf? Did he ever cry or anything before he rode?"

"Oh, no," Mom said. "The only time he cried was when he couldn't ride. I felt like crying a few times, especially when he was really young. Ty was fearless. He scared me to death more than once, but I never saw him scared. If he had been, I'd have told him not to ride."

I must have been a pistol, because I begged my dad to let me ride a calf when I was two years old. He and Mom both thought I was too young, and in hindsight, I would never recommend sticking a two-year-old on a calf. But I was a strong-willed kid, and I knew what I wanted. I begged and pleaded until, finally, Dad took me out to the corral and put me on the smallest calf he could find. With my free hand on Dad's back, and his right hand securely around my belt, we ran around the pen with Freckles leading the way to keep the calf ducking and diving. Dad swears he never held me on—that he was just there to break my falls—but he was there, and that was all that mattered.

Every day I'd beg Mom and Dad to let me ride, and most days they obliged. Mom would open the gate and count, "One alligator, two alligator, three alligator . . ."—all the way to eight before blowing an imaginary whistle. When it looked like I might not make it through the full eight seconds, she would speed up the count. I was two years old and didn't know any better. I thought I never fell off before reaching the time. No sooner had Mom tooted her make-believe whistle than I was saying, "Can I go again, Dad? Pleeeease. Just one more." Dinner was on the stove and my sisters were waiting, but more often than not he would say, "All right. One more."

As a kid you never fully appreciate those moments. As an adult, I realize what wonderful parents I have, and I thank them every day for the sacrifices they made for all of us.

During that time, I also rode an old Appaloosa named Doc. He was the perfect horse for a little squirt like me, calm enough not to cause any trouble, and smart enough to teach me a thing or two. At age two, I couldn't remember the barrel-racing pattern, even after my mom had drawn it out for me in the dirt. But Doc remembered. When I tried to steer him the wrong way, he would shake his head and stick to the right pattern. I would yell at him and spur him, madder than a hornet, until Mom pointed out that Doc was right and I was wrong.

Everything I did was geared around becoming a rodeo cowboy. I don't remember ever wanting anything else, even for a day. There was never a moment I said to anyone, "Maybe I'll be an astronaut," or, "I'd like to be president someday." I never even thought it. I arranged the sheets on my bed so they would hold my feet flat with my toes pointed out, a key position in bull and bronc riding. I convinced myself that if I slept that way while I was growing, I would be a better rider.

When I was seven, I watched the Montreal Olympics on our grainy RCA television, and I took particular interest in the gymnastics. "That's the kind of athlete it takes to be a great rodeo champion," I told my parents. "If I could balance like that and get strong like those guys, it'd sure help my riding." So, I took gymnastics; I learned to ride a unicycle; and I learned to juggle, not because I had an interest in being a gymnast or a circus clown, but because I knew those things were going to make me a better rider.

Everything I ate, drank, said, and thought centered on being a cowboy. And my family supported and encouraged me every step of the way.

Our family outings were trips to rodeos. Dad rode every weekend, and Mom's brother continued to compete and win the whole time I was growing up. Oddly enough, I remember attending rodeos as a toddler where my dad was riding, but I can't remember seeing him ride. Maybe I was too caught up in the surroundings to pay attention, or maybe I couldn't see that well, but I don't remember watching Dad at a rodeo.

I do remember my uncle Butch winning his first steer wrestling championship. When he showed me that gold buckle, I thought it was the most beautiful thing I'd ever seen. "I can't wait to get mine," I said to him. At the time everyone thought that was cute. There was no "if" or "maybe."

Before I could win my first championship, I had to win

my first rodeo. That day came when I was five years old. By then, I'd been riding calves for three years. While other kids my age were taking the training wheels off their bicycles, I traveled with my family to Camp Verde, Arizona, where I competed against twenty other kids in calf riding. Like most rodeos, there was a long round, then a short round for the contestants who qualified. The first night I was the only kid who stayed on until the whistle, which meant I won the event in the first round. That night my dad told me I had won, but I would have to ride the next day anyway. "Why can't they just give me the buckle now?" I asked. Today, of course, I understand. It would be like calling a football game at halftime because one team had a hundred-point lead. The event had to go on even though the outcome was decided. But at the time it seemed like a good question to me.

I made it to the whistle in the short round, too, even though it didn't matter in terms of the win. I couldn't have cared less. Every ride was important to me, and I kept that attitude throughout my career. Whether I was so far down in points that I had no chance of winning, or so far ahead that nobody could catch me, I rode the same way every time—all out, leaving nothing in the chute.

Later that afternoon, the rodeo organizers presented me with my first buckle and a $39 check. I tried to give them the check back, because I was sure it must have been a mistake. Why would anybody pay me to ride? I would have paid them every penny I could scrounge to do it all over again that day. That $39 must have been for somebody else. All I wanted was the buckle. Later, when I realized that I had, indeed, earned my first check as a rodeo rider, I gave it to my dad and said, "Here, Dad, let's go buy a Winnebago and a CB."

From that point on, my life revolved around rodeo. Not all of the experiences were as picture-perfect as that first one in Camp Verde. I was bucked off more than a few times. One bad weekend in Nogales, Arizona, the sun beat down, it was 110 degrees and dusty, and the dust didn't taste very good. I knew, because I ate more than my fair share that weekend. Amateur stock that wasn't as tough as what I'd ridden at home bounced me off the fence, then slammed me and hooked (or head-butted) me. It was frustrating, and I got angry. But I never gave up. Getting bucked off and hooked was part of the sport. I didn't have to like it, but I had to learn from those experiences.

I rode my first bull when I was nine years old, which is *way* too young for anybody to get on a bull. Usually junior rodeos have age brackets. Nine-to-twelve-year-olds ride steers, thirteen-to-fifteen-year-olds ride bulls that are old and don't buck very hard, and sixteen-to-eighteen-year-olds ride the big bulls. This gives a kid an opportunity to stair-step his way into the sport. But on occasion things don't work out. Dad and I went to a junior rodeo in Phoenix that had advertised steer riding. When we got there, all they had were bulls. "Sorry, Ty," Dad said. "We'll have to sit this one out."

"Pleeeeeease, can I ride, Dad?" I begged. "I can do it. I know I can."

Not in a million years was my dad going to put a nine-year-old on a bull. But I was persistent. Finally, the contractor got involved. He assured Dad that this was a gentle old brindle that was essentially harmless. "Well . . . ," Dad said. "If you think it'll be all right."

"He'll be fine," the contractor said.

Sure enough, I was fine. The big old brindle had horns that looked like tree limbs, but, as promised, he just loped along, occasionally darting and dipping, but not doing much. I made the whistle easily, which was the worst thing that could have happened to me. When I jumped off, I was convinced I was a big-time, full-fledged nine-year-old bull rider. It wasn't that hard. I could probably beat some of the big boys.

Later that year, still full of myself from that earlier ride, I got on a young bull that wasn't quite as understanding as the first one. I stayed on about seven seconds before being thrown onto my back. When I hit the ground, the bull stepped on my face and I heard something pop underneath my ear. It sounded like a firecracker had gone off. As soon as I stood up, my dad was at my side asking me if I was all right. I realized I couldn't speak. My face hurt worse than it ever had before.

Mom took me to see a local doctor. He took one look and said, "Uh-oh. Looks like you've broken your jaw, Ty."

Mom groaned. "Wires?" she asked.

The doctor nodded. I didn't know it at the time, but I was about to have my mouth wired shut. Then the doctor knelt down to break the news to me: "Now, Ty, we're going to take you back here and give you a little something to put you to sleep."

He was trying to explain the procedure in kid-friendly terms, but I grew up around animals. Putting something to sleep had a totally different meaning. I jumped straight up out of the chair and started for the door, shouting, "It's not that bad. I swear, it's not that bad." Surely, I thought, they would keep me around for breeding or something.

The doctor had no idea what I was doing, but Mom knew. "No, Ty," she said. "Not that kind of sleep."

Two weeks later, with my mouth wired shut and a helmet perched on my head, I won the junior rodeo finals. Pain and sacrifice were part of the price of winning. Even at nine, it was a price I was more than willing to pay.

MY FORMATIVE YEARS couldn't have been better. We weren't rich by any means, but we were closer than most families. During the week I'd ride Doc in the round pen, then, as the sun was setting, Dad and I would play cowboys and Indians with squirt guns. In the winter I would go with Dad to the racetrack, where we would exercise the horses that had bad histories in the gates. We would start so early you couldn't see the dirt beneath your feet, galloping the tough horses side by side, trying to beat each other in five-hundred-yard races. We would ride all day, then spend our nights with Skoal in our cheeks and rodeo videos or *The Outlaw Josey Wales* on the television.

Every weekend we loaded up the family and traveled

to rodeos. Our first mode of transportation was an old green horse van. We'd shovel the manure out and make beds for everybody. Then we upgraded to a small camper. Mom and Dad had one single bed, and my sisters and I shared the other. Later we progressed to a motor home. Mom would save $15 out of her weekly grocery money every week for entry fees. Sometimes in the summers, Dad would have to stay home and work extra so we could afford that week's rodeo. Plenty of times he worked all day, then drove all night to watch my sisters and me compete before turning around and driving all night again to be back at work. Dad would tell us stories every night about the old West, and I would lie in the middle of the small bed and imagine myself riding with Buffalo Bill, Jim Shoulders, and, my idol, Larry Mahan. We were all from different generations, but that didn't stop a kid from dreaming.

I also dreamed of what life must have been like for my great-grandpa and his brothers on the 101 Ranch. It couldn't have been better than this, I decided.

"YOU KNOW," I said to the reporter as the crowd noise from the PBR event echoed through the corridor, "a college kid was driving me back to my hotel at an event I was attending and we struck up a conversation. She said she was a senior in college, so I asked her what she wanted to do once she graduated. She said, 'I have no idea.' I know that's more common than you'd think, but it always astounds me. Here's a girl in her twenties who's about to graduate from college and she doesn't have a clue what she wants to do with her life. I can't comprehend that. I've always known what I wanted from the day I was born."

There was long moment of silence, the kind of pause reporters use to see if their subjects have anything more to say. "I love everything about the cowboy life," I said, filling the void before he turned off his tape recorder. "I've always loved it. There's no feeling in the world like making great rides on great animals. But my goal has never been to be a good roughstock rider. I've always wanted to be known as a great cowboy, a good, tough cowboy whose word still means something, and who lives his life in the cowboy way. I don't care about going down in history as a great bull rider or bronc rider. I just hope that when people think back after my career's over, they'll remember me as a great cowboy."

The reporter nodded and turned off the recorder. "Thanks, Ty. That just about covers it."

2

The King and I

MY MOM LOVES to tell the story about when I was ten years old and one of my neighbors saw me getting out of the truck on Sunday after getting back from a rodeo. My neighbor yelled over, "How'd you do in the rodeo, Ty?" I said, "I did all right." Later that night, as we were in the kitchen getting ready for dinner, Mom said, "Ty, why didn't you tell Kay that you won this weekend?" I said, "Mom, if you're good, you don't have to tell anybody."

I'm not alone in thinking that way. You won't find a lot of chest thumping from anybody in rodeo. The sport is too humbling. But beyond that, I've always enjoyed being anonymous. Even today, I like going out to eat and being treated no different from the folks I'm eating with. It's just the way I was raised. Dad and Mom made sure we always knew that, no matter what we did in rodeo or anything else, we were no better or no worse than anybody else. And if we ever thought any differently, they were around to bring us back down to earth.

Sometimes being anonymous worked out pretty well for me, especially as a kid. When we were on the road with the other traveling rodeo families, the kids would get together and have roping contests. I was small and not well-known, so nobody considered me much of a threat. We would play the roping equivalent of basketball's HORSE or PIG, where you matched the trick of the person ahead of you or you were out of the game. I'd mess around a little, missing the dummy a couple of times to get the rest of the kids feeling like they had me beat. Then I'd say, "Hey, you want to bet a buck on this next one?" Mom nicknamed me Bet-a-Buck, because I'd always come in with a wad of ones in my pocket after these sessions. Unfortunately that sort of anonymity doesn't last long. Word quickly spread that you didn't want to "bet a buck" with the little Murray kid.

At five feet nine inches tall and 170 pounds, I'm no giant today, but when I was thirteen years old, I looked as if I were nine. That was the year I made the jump from steer riding to bull riding. Mom would sit in the stands and hear people say things like "Look at that little kid on that bull!" or "Did you see what that young kid did tonight?" Those early rides were good, but they weren't spectacular. What made me stand out over the other riders was that I was so small. Seeing someone my size on a bull made you sit up and take notice. When I rode well, the "wow" factor increased.

Pretty soon I was getting my picture in the paper, and

reporters were interviewing me. I won the Arizona Junior Rodeo Association all-around titles in 1978 and 1979, and my picture first appeared in *Pro Rodeo Sports News* magazine when I was nine. By the time I'd hit my teens, features about me had shown up in most of the Arizona papers. Still, I didn't take any of it too seriously. If I didn't ride well, nothing else mattered.

I'd always known which direction I wanted to go in rodeo, and making the jump from steers to bulls confirmed it. I was a roughstock rider. Sure, I would continue to compete in the other events—bulldogging, calf roping, and team roping—but those were not the events I hoped to specialize in. I wanted to be a great all-around cowboy, which meant competing in all events. But my passion was in the roughstock events: bull riding, bareback riding, and saddle bronc riding. Those were the events I loved. There was only one problem: I'd never ridden a saddle bronc in my life.

Growing up, I'd always tried to emulate my dad. Whatever he did, I did. Whatever he rode, I rode. Dad never rode saddle broncs. He'd broken a thousand colts by the time I was thirteen, and I was helping him regularly in the breaking pen. But riding a bucking colt and riding a saddle bronc are two different things. Some of the biggest broncs weigh up to sixteen hundred pounds. The technique and physical requirements to ride them are nothing like those needed to break a colt. Because Dad had spent his rodeo career riding bareback and bulls, I spent my youth focused on those events as well.

Mom and Dad knew I wanted to expand into saddle bronc riding, so Dad gave me a job flagging the races at the tracks in New Mexico in the hopes that I could earn enough money to buy a bucking machine. I worked every day that summer and made a total of $840, a virtual fortune, or so I thought. Reality hit home when we got back to Arizona and Mom started making calls. "I've got a boy looking to buy a bucking machine," I heard her say into the phone. "Uh-huh. . . . Uh-huh. . . . Well, thanks anyway."

"What they say, Mom?" I asked.

She shook her head. "They have plenty of machines, but they cost between two thousand and six thousand dollars."

She might as well have said they cost a hundred million dollars. I thought $840 was huge. Two thousand was more money than my young brain could comprehend spending on anything. Looking back, that was a little pricey, even by today's standards. It was the *Urban Cowboy* era, and every struggling honky-tonk in Texas was installing a mechanical bull, so prices had jumped accordingly.

"Don't you worry," Mom said. She'd obviously picked up on my shock and disappointment. "I'll keep looking."

She scoured the papers every day and burned up the phone lines looking for a bargain. I'd almost given up when Mom found a classified ad that read, "Must Sell." As quickly as she could dial the phone, she had the owner on the line. He was recently married and in a financial bind. "I've got it listed for one thousand dollars," he said.

"Well," Mom said, "I've got a kid here who worked all

summer to buy one, and he's got eight hundred and forty dollars."

"Sold!" the man said.

Within a couple of days we had a bucking machine in the backyard. Dad and I put a saddle on it and I rode that machine until my thighs were raw. I put strips of cardboard inside my chaps when my legs started to bleed, but I wouldn't stop riding. Sometimes I'd go until midnight, programming the machine to randomly buck as fast and as hard as possible. I didn't hold back. I was just a kid, but I knew the bulls and saddle broncs I would be riding would be bucking with all they had, so I gave it all I had on that machine.

One evening Dad came home from the sale barn in Glendale with some interesting news: "I saw Larry Mahan at the sale today, and he asked about you."

I almost fell over. "You . . . you . . . Larry Mahan?" I said. I have no specific recollection of what I was wearing at the time, but there was a better than average chance it was Larry Mahan Western Wear. Larry was the King of Cowboys in my eyes. He was the sports idol I looked up to, the legend I aspired to emulate, and the man whose record I wanted to beat more than anything. Whatever Larry did, whatever he wore, whatever he rode, I wanted to copy him. Now Dad was telling me he had spoken with Larry, face-to-face, and The King had asked about me!

"Larry Mahan!" I said again. "What did he say?"

"He said he'd seen you ride, and he thought you had a lot of potential."

This was like having Joe Montana say, "You've got a good arm, kid." There was no greater praise in my eyes. "Did he say anything else?" I asked.

"Yeah." Dad paused.

What! What! I wanted to scream, but I had to play it cool. Dad was toying with me a little, and I knew it. I couldn't let him see how thrilled I was.

"I told him you were learning to ride saddle broncs. He said, 'Bring him out to the house and I'll help him.' " At the time, Larry had a place near Phoenix.

I had just been invited to the inner sanctum of the greatest cowboy in history. Larry had seen me ride—he'd watched me closely, or so I gathered—and now he wanted me to come to his place. Things were about to change. For once in my life I was thrilled that someone had remembered my name. You could throw fame out the window for all I cared. Larry Mahan thought I had potential. That was better than being named Man of the Year.

LARRY WAS THE FIRST cowboy celebrity, the first person to build a brand with his name outside of the sport. He was the first cowboy in history to win six PRCA all-around titles, and the only one to do it in roughstock events. He won his first bull-riding world title in 1965, and for the five years after that, nobody could touch him in the all-around. Larry was the first man in history to win five consecutive all-around titles, starting in 1966 and going through 1970. Injuries sidelined him for a couple of seasons in 1971 and 1972, but he came back strong in 1973, winning an unprecedented sixth all-around.

In his heyday in the 1970s, Larry appeared on television talk shows and made appearances with other athletes, guys like Don Meredith, Jerry West, Dave Marr, and Corky Carol. That was groundbreaking at the time. Nobody thought of rodeo cowboys as athletes, so to equate somebody like Larry with Jerry West was revolutionary. It was also a new experience for Larry. As he would later say, "I was pretty green and country back in those days. A good friend of mine, Marty Carmichael, who was the former attorney for the LPGA Tour, volunteered to help me with my contracts. This was before the days when cowboys had agents, and I really didn't consider Marty an agent. He was just a friend helping out."

Larry's world changed when another of Marty's clients, Dave Marr, suggested that Larry would make a fine addition to the Janzen sportswear team, a group of star athletes that promoted Janzen the same way Team Nike promotes products today. "A fellow named Roger Yost called and offered me a fifteen-hundred-dollar-a-year contract," Larry said. "Yost told me, 'Sorry, it's not much money,' but, hell, it was three times what I was making from my other endorsements. All of a sudden I was hanging out with the superstars of that time. There I was an old country boy who thought a stock split was when a cow had a calf, and I was listening to Jerry West and Don Meredith talk about what they were making in endorsements. It was unreal. That opened my eyes to what was possible. I knew I had to go out and tell the story of our sport, to promote the game and communicate what cowboys were all about to the outside world."

Larry starred in a movie called *The Great American Cowboy* in 1973. He certainly looked like a movie star. His hair was thick and wavy, fanning back away from his face like Eastwood's. He also had a rugged jaw and a great smile. The only problem was his acting. He spent a lot of time and money on acting lessons, and he continued to pick up bit parts throughout the seventies, but the acting career never panned out for him. Then he formed his own country-and-western band called Larry Mahan and His Rovin' Rodeo Review. They were awful, but I listened anyway. Just as I bought Larry Mahan Western Wear and his book, *Fundamentals of Rodeo Riding: A Mental and Physical Approach to Success.* In my eyes and in those of many others, he was the greatest rodeo cowboy in history. He was my Elvis, The King, the man who had brought rodeo into the mainstream, who had made it a sport, not just a curiosity or a sideshow. Larry had been the best roughstock rider in history. Then he'd become the most visible spokesman for American cowboys.

Now he was asking me to come out to his place to learn to ride saddle broncs.

I wanted to pick up the phone and call Larry that night. "No, Ty," Dad said. "It's nice when people compliment you and say things like 'Come see me,' but usually they're just being polite. They don't expect you to show up on their stoop."

I was crestfallen, but I figured Dad was right. He had been there. He had heard what Larry had said, and the way he had said it. If Dad thought Larry was just being polite, that he hadn't really meant it when he'd asked me out to his place, then that was the way we'd have to take it. Larry had told my dad that I had potential. Nothing could take that away. If I never met the great Larry Mahan, I was thrilled that he'd seen me ride, that he knew my name, and that he'd liked what he'd seen enough to tell my dad about it.

A few weeks later the phone rang at home and I answered it. "Hello."

"Ty," a cheery voice said. "This is Larry Mahan."

I froze for a moment, stunned. He sounded so . . . happy, normal, ungodlike. It was his voice, I knew. I'd seen *The Great American Cowboy,* and I'd always listened when he provided color commentary at televised rodeos. This was Larry Mahan all right, and I was standing in my parents' living room like a mute with the phone to my ear. "Yeah," I finally said. "What can I do for you, Mr. Mahan?"

"Well, if you want to learn how to ride saddle broncs, you can get your little butt down here. I told your dad to bring you down."

"Yes, sir," I said, struggling to keep up my end of the conversation. "We just thought . . . I don't know . . . We just figured you were being polite."

"I understand. One thing you need to know about me up

front: when I say something, I mean it. If I invite you down here, you're invited. Now, if you don't want to come—"

"No! No! I want to come! Yes, sir, I want to come down to see you as soon as possible."

So Mom, Dad, and I loaded up in the truck and rode down to Larry's place in Phoenix. He showed me a little about positions and techniques, about where to put my saddle and how to use the rein, and he told dozens of stories about his days in the arena. It was a fantastic time. In hindsight, he didn't teach me much about riding. But I left his place feeling like I'd been schooled by the master.

A couple of weeks later I got another offer from Larry. He called and said, "Ty, why don't you come out to my ranch in Colorado, spend some time this summer with me."

This time I knew better than to assume he was being polite. "I . . . I don't know." I looked at my dad and saw the furrowed brow he always had when he was pondering something important. "Let me call you back in a couple of days," I said. I had recently qualified for the National High School Finals rodeo, the biggest and most prestigious junior rodeo in the country. I would probably be one of the only freshmen there, and certainly the only one who had qualified in bull riding. That was where the problem arose. If I went to National High School Finals, I couldn't go to Larry's ranch. Plus, I didn't know what Larry planned on having me do while I was there. Were we going to ride? Were we going to rodeo together? Was he going to teach me saddle bronc riding? For all I knew he wanted me to work as a ranch hand shoveling stalls.

"It's your choice, Ty," Dad said. He never let on at the time, but Dad wanted me to pass on the National High School Finals. I was fourteen, but I was still tiny. The bulls at that rodeo were not going to be small, old, or gentle. I would be competing against seniors, kids three and four years older than me who were a lot bigger and who had a lot more experience than I did. Another year to grow, Dad figured, and I would be in much better shape. He never said that to me. He would never have hinted it. This was my call, my choice, a decision no one else could make.

"I think I'll go with Larry," I said to Dad.

"That's good. I don't think you'll regret it."

MY FIRST MORNING in Colorado I was sleeping in Larry's bunkhouse, a twelve-by-twelve cabin that I shared with one of the ranch hands. The place was in Guffey, in the mountains outside Colorado Springs, and I thought it was the most beautiful place I'd ever seen. Larry hadn't owned it long, so he hadn't gotten around to building his big house. He lived in a small structure that had been on the ranch for fifty years, and I slept a few yards away in the thin, cool air of the bunkhouse. It seemed like the perfect summer spot for a kid of fourteen.

The mountain air left a touch of moisture on my sheets. I was sleeping so well I thought I'd died and gone to heaven. Then I heard him. "Get up! Get up! Get up!"

I sat up like I'd been shot. "What?" I said, my head

pounding. I saw Larry standing over me, dressed and frowning.

"Drop out of that bunk and give me fifty push-ups," he yelled.

I was too confused to speak, but speaking wasn't what he had in mind.

"Now!" he shouted.

I rolled out of my bunk and hit the floor. The sun was up, which meant it had to be after 6 A.M., but it felt like the middle of the night. I'd never been one to wake up with a smile on my face and a spring in my step, and, at fourteen, I was a typical teenager. I would sleep until midmorning if I could. Now I was on the cold wooden floor of a strange bunkhouse being forced to do push-ups.

Larry was on the floor right beside me, matching me push-up for push-up, and chewing me out with every breath. "I've already run three miles, showered, and dressed," he said. "You can't just lay around in the sack all day."

All day wasn't what I had in mind, but sleeping until seven would have been nice. Little did I know this was going to be my morning ritual for the next five weeks.

"We've got some colts we need to break," Larry said. Fine, I could hold my own in the breaking pen. I'd been doing it with my dad since I was old enough to put my foot in a stirrup.

"Sounds good," I said.

Larry just smiled. I should have known right then that this wasn't going to be your ordinary, run-of-the-mill breaking session.

Sure enough, the two colts were loco, bucking, kicking,

running, and being skittish when anything mo
we would do what I'd always done with Dad, v
take our time, let the colts get used to being arou
slowly introduce them to the blanket, then the sa   ...en
to the idea of having someone on them. Dad had gotten so
good at this process that colts rarely bucked with him, even
when he mounted them for the first time. But Larry had different ideas. On his horse, he trotted out into the pen and
roped one of the colts, pulling it close and snubbing it (holding its head in the crook of his arm). Then he put a blindfold
over its eyes. I had read about cowboys on the range in the
1800s breaking colts this way, but I'd never seen it. Imagine
my surprise when Larry said, "All right, Ty, put your bronc
saddle on this one, and let's give it a go."

I put my bronc saddle on the colt and climbed on. Then
Larry uncovered the colt's eyes, and we were off. The colt
bucked and kicked and spun, and I did everything I knew
how to do to stay on him. In rodeos you have to stay on for
eight seconds. When you're breaking a colt, you stay on as
long as you can. It couldn't have been more than a minute or
so until the colt quit bucking, but it felt like an hour. Larry
chased us down with fifty feet of rope, sometimes throwing
it over my head instead of the colt's. He finally roped him,
snubbed him, blindfolded him again; we unsaddled him and
did the same thing with the other colt.

My first week on the ranch I still didn't know what was
in store for me, but I knew one of my chores for the summer.
We—mostly *me*—were going to break those colts. I was a
little surprised that Larry didn't give me any riding advice

during this process. He just turned me loose, and we had a grand old time getting those colts ready to ride.

I didn't realize it at the time, but Larry did a lot of things that summer to test my mettle as a cowboy. This wasn't a *Karate Kid* experience where he taught me the moves and methods of the master. He did a lot of things that made me question his sanity. One morning he sent me out to gather up fifty head of steers, but rather than put me on any of the normal workhorses he had all over the ranch, he had me saddle up a $60,000 halter horse, a show horse with a high step and great gate-jumping skills. Talk about pressure! There I was, fourteen years old, gathering steers on a $60,000 show horse while the corral was full of $1,200 horses that would have been better for the job.

Many years later Larry would laugh about it and say "I love to see how people handle different situations, different kinds of pressure. That's what I was doing with Ty. I didn't teach him anything about riding, because there wasn't anything to teach. He knew how to ride. I just wanted to teach him how to handle himself in different situations, how to react, and adapt to whatever came his way." Nobody was laughing that night when the halter horse turned up colicky. I was a nervous wreck, even though there was nothing I could have done to prevent it. A horse's digestive tract is so sensitive he can colic on you without warning, which is exactly what happened. "Oh, God," I said to myself. "I'm barely here a week and I'm going to kill a sixty-thousand-dollar horse." I could see the concern on Larry's face too. We had to keep the horse standing to keep him from rolling over and twisting his intestines, which was a shortcut to death for the animal. "Get in the back of that trailer and keep him up," Larry said. The nearest vet was forty miles away down a washboard dirt road, but I rode in the back of a trailer keeping this horse upright, and praying every mile of the way. Fortunately, the horse recovered, but not before I lost my appetite and several hours of sleep.

My next test came a few days later when Larry told me we were going to the White Mountains to speak to a summer camp of troubled Navajo children. "Rodeo is the sport of the Navajo nation," he said. "These kids look up to cowboys the way inner-city kids in L.A look up to Magic Johnson." I didn't really understand why I was there. Okay, so I was going with him to some camp for kids: all that meant to me was a day away from the ranch, and my first trip on an airplane.

Larry had a Cessna 310, a single-engine plane he had been flying for years. One of the funniest and most legendary stories about Larry came as a result of his buying this airplane. In the 1970s, nobody flew to rodeos. Cowboys drove their own trucks or rode with other cowboys, pulling their own trailers and lugging their own gear. Right after Larry bought the Cessna, he decided to fly himself to the rodeo in Pampa, Texas. As he was on approach to the Pampa airport, he radioed ahead and asked the FBO operator to phone the rodeo office and see if somebody could pick him up. A lady named June Ivory, who had been with the PRCA for years and who didn't take anything off any of the cowboys, took the call. When the airport manager radioed back to Larry, he said, "We've got a little problem." Larry asked what the problem was. After a moment of hesitation, the manager said, "Ms. Ivory said, and I quote, 'Tell that little sumbitch that if he can afford to fly, he can afford to take a cab from the airport.' "

Times had changed, but Larry still insisted on flying himself in his Cessna to most of his events. I'd never flown before in my life, so it was a thrill for me to sit in the right seat of a single-engine plane. We took off, and I watched everything Larry did. "This is the airspeed indicator," he said, pointing to one of the dials. "And this is the altimeter. It shows you how high you are, and if you're climbing or descending."

This was great. He wouldn't tell me anything about riding a bull or a bucking horse, but I was getting a handy lesson on the ins and outs of flying. "Your yoke is here, and this is the throttle," he said while showing me the wheel and a handle that I'd already figured increased engine power. "This dial here is the artificial horizon." He pointed to a blue-and-white bubble in a metal case. "It shows you what your attitude is. That means if you're tilted one way or the other, or if you're climbing or falling, you can see it with this dial."

I nodded, having no idea what was coming next. "Okay," Larry said. "You take the wheel. Keep the artificial horizon straight and level. That means don't let us go up or down, and don't pitch us one way or the other. I'm going to take a little nap. The aircraft is yours."

At first I thought he was kidding. But before I could say anything like "No, thanks, Larry, I think I'll pass," he leaned back in his seat, turned his back to me, and closed his eyes. I grabbed the wheel and looked at every dial, gauge, and button in that cockpit. I was too short to have a clear view out the windshield, so I stretched my neck to look out over the horizon. Nothing but blue skies and some mountains in the distance, but that didn't slow down my heartbeat. The plane wanted to climb, so I applied a little pressure to the yoke and forced it down. Then I'd get it too far down and pull it up a little. A little turbulence bumped us around, so the bubble in the artificial horizon wobbled, and I tried to correct it. Every second or two I glanced over to Larry to see if he was asleep, awake, dead, or just plain crazy. This couldn't have gone on for more than five minutes, but it felt like five hours. Finally, he stretched, yawned, and sat up. "Well, how'd you do?" he said.

"Pretty good, I guess," I said. "We're still up here."

He laughed. "Yeah, we are." He took back control of the plane. He never mentioned that flight again for fifteen years. Then, out of the blue, he told a reporter who had heard the story, "Ty saw my right eye was closed, but he couldn't see that my left eye was on the gauges." He was right, I couldn't. It took a reporter asking the question for him to finally say, "I just wanted to test his mettle a little bit. I knew he could ride bulls, but I wanted to see how he did on something he'd never seen before."

I guess I passed, but the tests weren't over yet. After we landed in the White Mountains and caught a ride to the Navajo camp, I sat near the front of the auditorium and listened to Larry give his speech. "Rodeoing is a lot like life," he said. "It's all about the man in the mirror, the choices he makes, the dedication he has, and the way he reacts to change.

"If you make a mistake in rodeo, it's yours. There's nobody you can blame it on, and nobody else who can make it better. There's only you.

"I've gotten a lot of great press in this sport over the years—some of it you have probably seen or read yourselves—but I learned a long time ago that if you start reading and believing your own press clippings, you're done. People are going to say good things about you, and they're going to say bad things about you. Some of it might be true, some not. But there was only one person who controlled the outcome of a ride when I was in the chute: me. And only one person can control the outcome of your life, no matter what the future brings. That person is you."

The place went nuts. Larry got a standing ovation from the kids, who yelled and shouted to him for a couple of minutes before things quieted back down. "Now," he said, "I would like to introduce a great American cowboy, somebody you should all get to know, because you're going to be hearing a lot more from him in the years ahead. Please welcome Ty Murray."

What? He wanted me to speak? I'd been listening to him, enjoying the cool afternoon, and thinking about our earlier plane ride. Not in my wildest dreams did I think I was coming here to speak. What was he thinking? What was he doing? And what was I going to do now?

Larry motioned me up to the podium, and I felt my legs carrying me to the front of the room. Counting counselors and special guests, there had to be three hundred people in this auditorium, all of them looking at me. What was going through their minds? How many of them were saying, "Who the devil is this kid?"

I stood before them and talked for a couple of minutes, reiterating a lot of the points I'd just heard come out of Larry's mouth, as well as some of the things I'd heard my dad say over the years. It wasn't much of a speech, but it was all you could expect from a fourteen-year-old kid on twenty seconds' notice. Afterward, Larry and I sat at the head table for an autograph session. The kids rushed him, hoping to get their hero's signature. Before they got to him, Larry reached into his pocket and pulled out an extra pen. "Here," he said, handing it to me.

"What's that for?" I asked.

"The autographs."

"Nobody's going to want my autograph."

"Yes, they will." And they did, mostly because Larry told all the kids, "Be sure and get Ty's autograph. You'll be glad you did someday."

I didn't have to fly the plane on the way back to the ranch, which was a good thing. I'd had enough tests for one day.

THE FOLLOWING WEEK I got some more news. "We're going to Colorado Springs for a rodeo," Larry said. "Well, it's more of an exhibition than a rodeo." By this time I knew to expect the unexpected. "We'll take those colts we've been breaking."

The colts in question had been on the ranch their whole lives. They were still pretty green on top of being loco. I wouldn't have taken them into Guffey if it had been up to me, but Larry said they were going to Colorado Springs, so we loaded them up and took them.

He was the celebrity MC for this event, and while I didn't know what my role was going to be, I knew he had something in store for me. An hour or so into the exhibition, I had my answer. "Now we're going to give you a little demonstration on the evolution of bronc riding," Larry said into his microphone. "Back in the 1800s, when Wild West shows were becoming a popular pastime in the Eastern cities, bronc riding was a lot different than it is today. To demonstrate what things were like back then, please welcome Ty Murray!"

So, this was it. We were going to blindfold the colt and ride him without a flank strap, just as we'd done back at the ranch. A guy named Mark who worked for Larry got on his horse, roped and snubbed the colt, and put the blindfold on him just as we'd done before. Then he motioned me out into the arena with my bronc saddle and halter. I climbed onto Mark's horse behind him and, from there, saddled up the colt and climbed on. Mark took off the blindfold, and once again, we were off. The colt bucked, then bucked and spun, then just spun until he got so dizzy he fell over on his side. I got off and the crowd cheered.

"Now," Larry said, "Ty will show us how saddle bronc

riding has changed over the years, and how it's done today."

There was only one problem: I knew what bronc riding looked like, but I wasn't sure how to do it. I'd only been on three saddle broncs in my life. Why wouldn't he get someone else who knew what he was doing to demonstrate modern bronc riding? I knew how to hang on to those colts we'd been breaking. I'd done it for most of the summer. But when it came to riding a flanked saddle bronc, where you had to lean back, set your feet, and spur back (cue the horse by pulling the spurs across his shoulders), I had no idea what I was doing. That was how Larry did things: seat of the pants to see how I handled it.

I did okay. I stayed on. The crowd didn't know this was the fourth saddle bronc I'd ever ridden, and they gave me a nice round of applause. It was another passing grade in Larry Mahan's cowboy tests of life.

I THINK BACK on that summer often, and the memories get happier with every passing year. Most nights Larry and I would sit outside with his ranch hands, cooking on an open fire, and watching the stars in the Colorado sky. Larry would break out the guitar and sing a few of his old-time favorites, and I would tell him it sounded like a coyote mating call. We'd laugh and tell stories, talk about horses and enjoy each other's company. I'll never forget those days, the things I learned, and the friendships I made while I was there.

We went to Miles City, Montana, toward the end of my summer stay for a celebrity team-roping exhibition. Larry, as he did with every trip, took me along for the ride. Larry was on a team with music legend Charlie Daniels, while Walt Garrison and a famous bronc rider named Bud Pauley were on the other team. Larry knew I roped, so before the exhibition he said, "Ty, why don't you have a go at them." By this time I was so used to Larry's putting me on the spot that I didn't hesitate. I jumped on the back of one of the biggest horses there and roped several steers right away. Those guys got a huge kick out of it, not just because I was able to rope the steers, but because I looked like a little kid sitting on the back of that huge horse. To this day, Charlie Daniels never lets me forget that story.

But the things I remember most about my time with Larry were the little lessons in life he taught me. If we were standing in a room full of people, Larry wouldn't strike up a conversation with the cowboys; he'd find the punk rocker or the college professor or the housewife and visit as though they were long-lost friends. He had a knack for making acquaintances with the most eclectic group he could find, and he never met a stranger. Years later he would admit that this wasn't by accident. "When I got into rodeo, it was a closed world," he said. "You had to look the part, dress the part, and act the part or cowboys wanted nothing to do with you. I saw what other sports were doing, and I knew that for rodeo to grow we had to reach out to others, to communicate what our sport was all about. That was the only way to increase our fan base and make it more attractive for everyone. Whenever I saw someone I thought I could win over to our sport, I talked to them. Hopefully my generation took us to another level.

"When I saw Ty, I knew he was going to be the one in his generation who could take it to yet another level. To do that, he had to represent the sport and speak to outsiders in a language they understood. I tried to teach him that, and he seemed to learn it pretty well."

When I got back home after a month and a half with Larry, my mom couldn't believe it. "You've grown a foot!" she said. "Butch, look how big he's gotten."

Dad nodded, but seemed less enthusiastic about my growth spurt. "Did you learn anything?" he asked.

I thought for a second before answering. "Yeah. I learned a lot." They just weren't the kinds of lessons I'd expected.

3

Growing Up Cowboy

AFTER A SUMMER with my hero, Larry Mahan, I'd learned a lot, but I still needed a lot more experience on saddle broncs. It wasn't something I'd done my whole life, and even though I'd spent six weeks with one of the greatest riders in history, I'd still only been on half a dozen saddle broncs. I could compete with anyone my age (and a fair number of kids a lot older than me) in bull riding and bareback riding, but to be a great roughstock rider I needed more experience saddle bronc riding. It wasn't enough to be good at two events and hope my skills in those masked my weaknesses in a third.

I also believed that being a great cowboy meant being a great horseman. That didn't mean I wanted to hop on a horse and make it go where I wanted it to go. Great horsemen understand and communicate with their animals. They can control a horse's movements without ever touching the reins, and there isn't a horse out there they can't ride. The quest for great horsemanship among cowboys dates as far back as the founding of our frontier. Meriwether Lewis wrote lengthy passages in his journal about the horse skills of the American Indians, of how they could fire their arrows from the backs of horses in full gallop, controlling the direction and speed of the animals with a slight change in pressure from their knees.

That was a tradition I had to continue: to be a great all-around cowboy I had to be a great all-around horseman.

Brad Gjermundson, a four-time World Saddle Bronc Riding Champion from North Dakota, hosted a bronc riding school at Estrella Park in Arizona, which I was desperate to attend. But the school cost $350, not a lot of money in today's dollars when you consider what some parents pay to send their kids to YMCA camps, but a pretty good investment in the early eighties, especially for a modest family with three teenage kids. Mom put away $5 a week from her grocery money, but when the deadline came for Brad's school, we only had $185.

Our break came when Mom got a call from the riding school. "Mrs. Murray, I understand your son has a bucking machine," the school representative said.

"That's right. It's in our backyard," Mom said.

"Well, we'd like to know if we can rent it for the school. We've been looking around for one, and they're pretty hard to come by."

It was all Mom could do to contain her glee. "Have we

got a deal for you," she said. Brad Gjermundson traded my tuition for use of my bucking machine, and Mom got to save her $185. Dad and I unbolted the machine and hauled it to town, where I spent the week learning the ins and outs of saddle bronc riding from a world champion.

My family always worked as a team like that. Even my sisters, who were older and, by every sibling right, could have been jealous of all the attention I got, were always supportive. Kerri was a good rodeo cowgirl. She earned a scholarship to Central Arizona College in Casa Grande, where she qualified for one national college final. The two of us would have roping contests in the backyard throughout our teenage years, and the competition could get intense. I remember one afternoon we were neck and neck, having both roped four calves in a row. On the fifth calf, Kerri, who is six years older than me, roped the calf perfectly, and I missed. For the rest of the day, I was her slave. I had to do everything she told me to do. I washed her dishes, cleaned her room, and brought her drinks when she was thirsty. When I was on the phone with friends, Kerri would say, "Hang up. I need a back rub," and I would have to tell my friends I'd call them back. It was a miserable afternoon, but I honored the bet. The only saving grace was the knowledge that Kerri wasn't as hard on me as I would have been on her.

My oldest sister, Kim, rodeoed until she was fifteen, but she enjoyed the social aspects of rodeos more than the actual riding and roping. Getting dirty and practicing became a chore for her, so Dad finally said, "Look, it's expensive to do this. If you don't want to give it a hundred percent, let's do something else. We'll support you in whatever you want to do, but let's not waste time and money if this isn't something you want."

I never got that speech, because I couldn't imagine doing anything other than riding. Everything I did revolved around rodeo. I continued to work out with the gymnastics team at Deer Valley High School, and I qualified for every meet, but I never went to an event. They always conflicted with rodeos. I didn't realize that was going to be the case when I went out for the team, and at times my mom would say, "Ty, why don't you just go to the gymnastics meet and see how you do," but I wasn't willing to sacrifice a rodeo weekend for anything. Even as a junior, you accumulate points toward national standings, and any rodeo I skipped would mean a missed opportunity to earn more points. It was never a hard decision for me. If I'd had to skip Christmas to be at a rodeo, I would have done it without thinking twice. Gymnastics was fun, and I enjoyed being on the team, but I looked at it as a way of training my body for rodeo, getting a sense of body control whether I was in the air, on the ground, or on an apparatus. It also made me stronger, quicker, and more flexible, all traits I needed to be a good rider.

Nor was I too torn up when my friends would call and ask me to go to football games. "No," I'd say, "I've got a rodeo in the morning. I've got to get some rest." At times my folks thought I wasn't a normal kid, but I thought I was the luckiest teenager in the world. I got to spend every weekend rodeoing. What could be better than that?

I went to the largest high school in Arizona, one with only about half a dozen other rodeo cowboys, so I didn't have a lot in common with most of the kids in school. One girl had a Mercedes 450SL with a vanity license plate that read 16 B'DAY. She and I were pretty far apart in our life experiences. But I didn't let that bother me.

I never let peer pressure interfere with my goals. As a result, I never, ever, experimented with drugs, even as a kid in the eighties when marijuana and cocaine were in high schools across America. This wasn't a tortured decision on my part. In fact, it was pretty easy.

When I was young—eleven or twelve—I saw, first-hand, the effects drugs could have on a cowboy's career. Two young cowboys, both sixteen, were considered up-and-comers in our area. I watched them the way any eleven-year-old kid watches a sixteen-year-old. They were adults in my eyes, and I thought they were world-class cowboys. They were also potheads. Everybody knew it, even the younger kids. One night after one of those boys had a great bull ride, he turned to the other and said, "Let's go burn one!" I was young, but I knew what he meant. As time went on, I saw those two guys—teenagers who had as much natural skill and ability as anybody at the time—move steadily downhill. Their talent waned; their reflexes slowed; their stamina weakened; and their ability to perform at a high level disappeared. They both went from being superstars in waiting to mediocre amateurs.

Sure, I saw plenty of drugs when I was a kid, and I've

seen plenty in my adult life, but I never used and had little use for those who did. When I was a senior in high school, like many seniors I had a party at my house when my parents were away. As often happens with gatherings of this type, some kids came over that I'd never seen before. One of them decided that my bathroom was the perfect spot to snort a few lines of coke. I walked in on him and promptly threw him out of my house. In addition to its being something I considered stupid, the illegality of having drugs around always scared me. What would it do to my rodeo life if I got caught in a drug sting, or if I was with somebody who was busted for possession? I didn't know and I didn't want to find out.

I hear a lot of talk today about kids being pressured to experiment with substances because they want to be "cool." That seems odd to me. When I was in school, I thought the kids who used drugs were anything but cool. Most of them were screwups, and the rest were so nondescript they didn't stand out at all. I knew what they looked like, what they acted like, and what they did with their lives, and I knew I didn't want to be like them. I never gave drugs a second thought.

As I got older, the question of drug use in rodeos continued to come up. Professional rodeo is a lot like the NFL. Athletes in our sport have to fight through injuries and play with pain. But the incentives for cowboys to ride while injured are greater than they are in most other sports. Unlike quarterbacks or shortstops, if a cowboy can't compete because of an injury, he doesn't get paid. That increases the incentive to push yourself whether it's naturally or through chemical enhancement. Painkillers are the most obvious avenue for potential abuse, but, believe it or not, few cowboys take them.

I've taken no more than five painkillers my whole life. When I'm riding with an injury, I want to know where I'm hurting, and what level of pain I'm experiencing, so I can adjust my technique. If I've somehow deadened my pain, I risk developing a more serious and potentially career-ending injury because I don't know what parts hurt or how bad the pain is. Even my worst injuries, the ones where the pain was so bad I saw white and thought I was going to pass out, weren't so bad that I resorted to drugs. White-hot pain like that only lasts a little while. If you've conditioned your body properly, your brain puts out its own painkillers.

Most cowboys look at drug use the same way I do. Rodeo is too fast, and the dangers are too great, to be drugged up. Riding a bull or a bucking horse is serious business. Critical mistakes can happen with lightning speed. If your reflexes are impaired, or your judgment is clouded, you can get killed in an instant. Anybody who gets into the arena when he's high or otherwise impaired isn't long for this sport.

RODEO IS SERIOUS business, and hard work, but I never want anyone to think I didn't have fun. If riding and competing hadn't been fun for me, I would never have done it. Some kids played music growing up, others enjoyed traditional high school sports like football, basketball, and baseball, while others just hung out and socialized. I had rodeo, something I loved more than eating or sleeping, something I could do with my family and friends. And it was something I was good at.

There were plenty of late nights, long rides, and occasional frayed nerves along the way, but I wouldn't have changed my teenage years for anything. One day, after a particularly long weekend in Kansas, Mom was just too tired to go on. We were on a long strip of Midwest road, the kind of stretch that can make you tired even if you've had a good night's rest. Mom couldn't drive the motor home another mile.

"I'll drive it," I said, all full of myself. I was fourteen at the time, a year away from being legally able to drive a car with adult supervision, but I didn't look a day older than twelve.

Fortunately, as I'd grown up with lots of horses and an arena in our backyard, Dad had taught me to drive when I was thirteen. He'd put the pickup truck in the arena and told me to drive it around in circles until I got a feel for it. This was pretty typical in many parts of the West, where kids had to help out on the ranch or run errands for their parents. Most cowboys I knew learned to drive when they were twelve or thirteen. They weren't being willful lawbreakers. It was just a necessity. I had gotten pretty good at driving a stick-shift pickup truck around an enclosed arena, so I didn't think anything about driving a Winnebago Indian, with a four-horse trailer attached, straight down a Kansas highway.

I never counted on the truck. It was a tandem eighteen-wheeler that looked nine feet wide from a distance, and it was barreling right toward us. He was on his side of the road, and I was successfully keeping the motor home on our side of the yellow line, but at the bottom of a small hill, at exactly the spot I calculated we would cross paths, was a tiny bridge. I didn't think two cars would fit across the bridge at once. A motor home and a semi had no chance. If I'd had a little more experience behind the wheel, I would have slowed down and let the truck pass. Instead I kept a steady speed with both hands on the wheel. When we both got to the bridge, I either closed my eyes or temporarily blacked out, because I never saw the truck go by. We couldn't have missed each other by more than an inch.

"Mom," I said, snapping her out of a nap. "I think you should drive now."

She continued to drive me everywhere, regardless of how far from home we traveled or how much she and my dad had to sacrifice. Mom would scour the *Rodeo News*, mapping out events I could enter and budgeting our money and travel time. We put 150,000 miles on that motor home, but nobody seemed to mind. At a rodeo in Iowa, Mom sat behind a couple of local men who didn't know who she was, but she knew exactly whom they were talking about. "Who is that kid?" one of them asked. The other said, "I don't know, but he must be good if he drove all the way from Arizona." Actually we'd driven from New Mexico. I wasn't sure what my ability had to do with how many miles we drove, but we saw a lot of the country in those early years.

I learned a lot about human nature during those travels. As I began winning more often, junior rodeo officials who were also parents tried to change some of the rules. First they wanted a rule that you couldn't count your points in all six events for the all-around, which was the title every kid (and every adult for that matter) wanted to win.

The all-around title, as the name indicates, goes to the cowboy with the most cumulative points in all events. If a guy only competes in one event, such as calf roping, he might win that event going away, but he's ineligible for the all-around title because you have to compete in two or more events to qualify. Guys who compete in three, four, five, or six events have more opportunities to earn points. It's like giving a bowler ten extra frames. He might not bowl the most strikes, but he doesn't have to.

In the junior ranks a lot of kids were good bull riders or bucking horse riders or ropers, but not many could compete at a high level in all six events. I could, so I won more all-around titles. The kids didn't like losing to me, but they understood that they were getting beat fair and square. It was the parents who tried to manipulate the system by changing the rules.

Someone also proposed that the age for bull riding be

upped from thirteen to sixteen, and that the thirteen-through-fifteen-year-olds should ride steers. If that passed, kids who specialized in roping would continue to ride steers for all-around points. They didn't want to be bull riders, but they wanted to earn more points and stay competitive in the all-around. Mom and Dad were convinced this idea was aimed squarely at me. I won more bull riding events than any other kid and also competed well in the timed events. That gave me a distinct advantage.

Finally, at one of the meetings where these rule changes were being discussed, an old man stood up in the back and said what my parents wanted to say: "The answer is simple. If you want to beat him, don't change the rules, just practice harder."

According to my dad, I won 181 saddles before turning pro. That included six World Little Britches titles—two bareback, two saddle bronc, and two all-around—and two National High School titles, the biggest and most prestigious national junior rodeo in the country. Every state was represented at the National High School Finals rodeo, with the top four cowboys in each event from each state qualifying. I didn't go to the event my freshman year (that was the summer I spent with Larry Mahan), but I made it the next three years.

The first two were in Rapid City, South Dakota, and once again, Mom drove me up in the motor home. My senior year, the event moved to Pueblo, Colorado, and Dad got to see me ride. It wasn't easy on him. He had to work the races in New

Mexico in the morning, then hop in his truck and drive 350 miles to Pueblo. After watching me ride, he hopped back in the truck and drove all night back to New Mexico. He repeated that process for three straight days. By the last one he was whipped. But when I won the bareback and all-around titles, nobody could have been happier than my dad.

They gave me a buckle with National Champion on it for winning the all-around title at the National High School Finals, which meant more to me than any saddle or buckle I'd ever before won. Winning Little Britches titles was great, but those events were more regional. They might have called it the Little Britches World Title, but probably less than a dozen states and only one or two Canadian provinces were represented. The National High School Finals brought in the best of the best from all over the country. I won against guys from Alaska, Hawaii, Maine, and every state in between. For a kid, that win was as big as it got.

It also gave me a lot of self-confidence when it came to picking a college. I had received a lot of scholarship offers from colleges around the country. Most Western schools fielded rodeo teams, just as most Eastern schools competed in crew and lacrosse. I had plenty of choices, but I chose to go to Odessa College in Texas, where I'd been offered a full rodeo scholarship, and a chance to lead the team to a national championship. Odessa had just graduated Jim Sharp, a champion bull rider and someone I looked up to as a role model. Going to the school Jim was leaving was both a great honor and a big challenge.

Still I was pretty lucky. I was only seventeen years old and I had everything I needed: a 1980 Ford, three-quarter-ton pickup, a horse trailer, a college scholarship, and $3,000 in additional scholarship money I'd won in Little Britches (although we had to make a few calls to get that money since I'd gotten a full ride from Odessa). What more could a kid need?

.Mom and Dad dropped me off in Texas six weeks before my eighteenth birthday. Mom called it the toughest day of her life. Dad summed it up perfectly when he said, "Weaning is for the mare, not the colt." As for me, I was out on my own for the first time and loving every second of it. Life couldn't have been much better.

RODEO IS THE ONLY sport where you are allowed to compete at the collegiate level and professionally at the same time. Because of that rule, there was never a question about when I would turn pro. The Professional Rodeo Cowboys Association wouldn't issue a permit (or riding license) to anyone under eighteen, so I had to wait until October. Then, as a surprise for my eighteenth birthday, Mom and Dad drove from Albuquerque to Vernon, Texas, where I was competing in a college rodeo. They brought a notarized copy of my birth certificate, so I could get my PRCA permit.

This didn't mean I could ride in any rodeo I wanted. The odd thing about rodeo is that although you had to be eighteen to get a permit to ride, that didn't mean you were any good. Anybody off the street with $200 who could prove he was over eighteen years old could get a PRCA permit, even if he'd never been on a bucking animal in his life. Of course he'd get killed in his first rodeo, but that was our way of weeding out those who didn't belong.

As for getting into rodeos, full-fledged card-carrying PRCA members take priority over guys who are simply riding on a permit. Think of it like a temporary visa: A rider gets a permit, which gives him the right to enter any rodeo where openings are available. He must then earn a specific amount of money (then $2,500) in a season to buy his "card" or membership into the PRCA.

Once a cowboy has proved himself by earning a card, he has greater standing than non-card-holding riders, but he still can't get into every rodeo. The top performers, in our case the leading money winners, take priority. Once those top earners enter, other card members fill the rest of the field. If space is still available, permit holders are allowed to enter. If permit holders don't fill the field, or somebody who has signed up to compete doesn't show up, local guys and amateurs are allowed to ride as "turnouts."

I went to a lot of rodeos as a kid hoping to get a turnout. Rodeo contractors wanted to show off their bucking stock to the crowds even if there wasn't a card-carrying cowboy around to ride, so organizers paid $10 for every turnout ride. I couldn't have cared less about the money. Hell, I would have paid them $10 to ride. I wanted the experience of riding good stock in front of good crowds.

I'd had that chance one night in Phoenix when, as a sixteen-year-old, I got on a turnout saddle bronc called Five Spot. He was an "eliminator," a hard bronc to make a good ride on. I didn't know the horse's reputation at the time. I thought I was lucky that he'd been turned out.

I was also lucky that an old family friend and professional cowboy, Cody Lambert, was in the crowd that night. Cody's father had worked in the racing industry with my dad for a number of years when Cody was a teenager and I was a baby. Our families had known each other for years, although I knew Cody more for his reputation as a great professional cowboy than as a friend of the family.

When the chute opened, Five Spot proved himself. He was definitely harder to ride than any other bronc in the competition that night. I put together one of the best rides of my young career. After the ride the crowd stood and applauded, and I knew I'd put on a good show. A tough-looking cowboy with a bushy Fu Manchu mustache found me behind the chutes.

"You remember me?" Cody asked.

"Sure," I said, although I didn't really remember him as much as I knew who he was.

"When you get your PRCA card, give me a call," he said. "We'll rodeo together."

Later that night I rode a turnout bull on which Cody had ridden earlier that week to win the bull riding title. I had another great ride, one I hoped Cody had seen. He was already gone, but he heard about it the next week.

A group of cowboys who had been in Phoenix stopped

him and said, "Hey, Cody, we saw a high school kid ride that bull you won on in Phoenix. You better be glad he was a turnout and not in the competition or you'd have gotten beat."

"Was his name Ty Murray?" Cody asked.

The cowboys couldn't remember, but Cody knew.

Now I had my permit, which put me one step closer to getting my card and competing in the big leagues. It was mid-October of 1987, which meant I was running out of time to get my card for the 1988 season. I only had eight weekends before the end of the year, and some of those were out because of school commitments. If I was going to be a PRCA cowboy, I needed to do some serious riding in a short time.

MY FIRST PROFESSIONAL event was in Dayton, Ohio, the first weekend in November 1987. My college coach's son, Todd Watkins, and I drove from Odessa, in southwest Texas, to Dayton, in southwest Ohio, a full day on the road. It turned out to be one of the most important trips I'd ever make. I'd never been to Ohio, and outside the Browns, Indians, Bengals, and Reds, I didn't know much about the place. But location didn't matter. Wherever I went, I knew I had to ride well there to have any shot at my card.

Luckily, I got into all three roughstock events (saddle bronc, bareback, and bull riding). If there had been more cardholders in Dayton, I might have gotten into only one, two, or none of the events, but with the season winding down and most professionals having ridden in over one hundred rodeos by November, Dayton had a pretty light field.

That's not to say the stock was easy. I had a pretty tough bull that I rode really well, and I did okay on both my bareback draw and in the saddle bronc competition. By the end of the weekend, I had won the bull riding, placed second in the bareback, and finished third in the saddle bronc riding. My total take was $1,473.62, more money than I could have imagined earning for a day's work.

Monday morning I called the PRCA office, where I spoke with a nice lady named Bea. "I just won fourteen hundred seventy-three dollars and sixty-two cents," I said to Bea. I was sure to include the correct change. "How much more do I need to earn to get my card?"

"Let's see." I could hear her punching calculator keys. "You still need one thousand twenty-six dollars and thirty-eight cents."

"Okay. I'm going to California for a couple of rodeos. I'll call you when I've got enough."

She laughed. "You do that, honey." Bea had obviously heard this before. Kids just didn't earn their cards in three quick trips. If I thought this was going to be easy, I had a lot of learning ahead of me.

But I knew what I had to do. I drove home to Phoenix for Thanksgiving. Then Mom, Dad, and I loaded up the truck and headed for the Pacific Coast, to Costa Mesa, California, for my second professional start.

It's amazing how your perspective changes as you

grow. That November, I thought the Costa Mesa rodeo was huge. It was a professional rodeo, the Big Time, and I was there competing in the most important event of the year for me. Later in my career, I realized that the Costa Mesa rodeo was as small as they come, a rodeo I couldn't imagine attending again. It was staged on an old ice-skating rink in the Orange County Fairgrounds, where organizers covered the ice with dirt and installed temporary fencing and chutes. Unfortunately for me, even though the Costa Mesa rodeo was second-tier at best, it was also popular. Bull riding and saddle bronc events had been filled with cardholders. Bareback riding was all I could enter.

The horse I drew was huge, which worked to my advantage. Although I was eighteen, I was still fairly undeveloped. I didn't need to shave, so I looked like a kid on a giant bucking horse, which played well to the judges. Plus, in addition to bucking, this horse spun, which usually meant more points if you rode him well.

Roughstock events are judged, just like figure skating and diving, and the same elements of human nature enter into the judging. Three judges, all cowboys, judge a ride giving a total of fifty possible points for the animal (the bull or bucking horse) and fifty possible points for the rider. To get a score, a rider has to stay on the animal for eight seconds. If you're thrown before the eight-second whistle, you "no score," which means you don't get a score for that ride. Once you make it the full eight seconds, the score you earn depends on the quality of the ride and the quality of the animal.

While we've never had any judging scandals in rodeo like they've had in figure skating, arguments are bound to happen. Anytime a subjective human element is injected, there are bound to be disagreements. These disputes can get pretty heated. After a few years of having their judges abused and threatened, the PRCA passed a rule that any cowboy who cussed at a judge would be fined. One rider who felt that he'd been shorted a few points tested the limits of that rule when he asked one of the judges, "Would I get fined if I called you a stupid son of a bitch?"

"Yep," the judge answered.

"Well, what if I just thought you were a stupid son of a bitch? Could you fine me?"

The judged scratched his chin for a second, then said, "No, I can't fine you for thinking something."

"Good," the cowboy said. "Then I think you're a stupid son of a bitch."

That story has been passed around and laughed at in rodeo circles for years, but it illustrates an important point: judged events are only as good as the people judging them. I was fortunate in Costa Mesa. The judges didn't know me and had no preconceived ideas about how I was supposed to ride. All they saw was a scrawny-looking kid who could easily have passed as a seventh-grader climbing onto a huge rank bareback.

The horse was old and smart, the kind of animal that tries to teach all new kids a thing or two. Later in my career we joked that horses like that had been around so long they could hum the national anthem. I did what I usually did with the older, smarter horses, taking charge in the chute and letting him know from my body language that, despite my size, I was in charge. I didn't mean to cause him any trouble, and I didn't expect any trouble out of him. If he'd been young or scared, I would have treated him differently, petting him and letting him get used to me before I ever introduced him to my rigging. But you had to strike a deal with the older ones before the chute ever opened. I hoped I had done that.

The less time in the chute the better. Once you're over a bucking animal, only a few things can happen, and not many of them are good. I didn't want to rile this horse any more than I had to in those close confines, so I worked my gloved hand under the handle of my bareback rigging (a hard rawhide handle that looks like a suitcase handle on top of a leather and neoprene strap) all the way to my palm, above my calluses, then cracked the front of my hand out slightly. This gave me my "bind," which is the connection between the glove and the rigging, stronger than a mere grip. Throughout my riding career I worked on strengthening my bind, designing gloves and riggings that almost melded together like one piece when I put my hand in the right position. This time I was just happy to find the bind quickly so as to get out of the chute before the big horse caused me any trouble.

I gave the gate men a quick, curt nod, and the chute flung open.

My riding arm was straight, and I was leaning back and

lifting as hard as I could on my rigging. From this position the only way the horse could jerk my butt off the rigging is if he somehow tore my arm off. I also moved my feet up and over the break of the horse's shoulders. Bareback riding has something called a "spur out" rule where a rider's spurs have to be over the points of the horse's shoulders before his front feet hit the ground the first jump out of the chute. I set myself up for the spur out by turning my toes out and placing my spur shanks in front of the horse's neck.

This horse jumped out quickly and immediately began to spin. Usually a quick-bucking, spinning horse won't allow you to get much "exposure" where your legs are out and you are lying back as the horse peaks. But I had full exposure on this ride. It was as strong a performance as I'd had in quite some time.

The older guys judging the event were impressed. They'd never expected to see a kid ride a horse that big as well as I rode him. The scores reflected their surprise. At the end of the weekend I'd won the bareback competition.

That moved me within a couple hundred dollars of what I needed for my card. Our next stop was 250 miles north in Clovis, California, right outside Fresno. This time I got in all three events, which allowed me to breathe a little easier. If I rode reasonably well in two out of the three events, I was certain to earn enough money for my card.

I put together another good bareback ride, this time on a smaller—but equally rank—horse than the one in Costa Mesa. Winning the bareback riding, the first event of the weekend, sealed the deal. I had done it! In three rodeos, I had earned enough money for my PRCA card, which meant I had a better shot at getting in the good professional rodeos in 1988. I was thrilled.

After my ride, as I was soaking up the atmosphere in the arena, a gruff voice brought me back to earth. It was Cotton Rosser, the cranky rodeo contractor who had provided stock for the Clovis rodeo. Rodeo contractors aren't much different from racehorse breeders in what they do for a living. Cotton and others specialized in breeding and raising bucking stock, purifying bloodlines, selling semen, and campaigning their prize stock at as many top-notch rodeos as possible. But as far as personalities go, bucking stock contractors are on a different planet compared to their counterparts in horse racing.

Cotton was a perfect example. "Hey, kid," Cotton shouted. "Can you ride a horse?" Because I'd won the bareback competition, I had to make a victory lap on a saddle horse.

I was so happy with my win I wasn't going to let a surly old hard-ass like Cotton bring me down. "I can ride one for eight seconds," I said.

Even Cotton got a laugh out of that.

I placed in all three events in Clovis, which pushed me well over the limit for my card. Mom and Dad were the first to congratulate me. "I knew you would do it," Dad said.

"Well, I'm glad *you* did," I said. "Thanks for not telling me."

The next morning, with the truck loaded and ready for

the trip back to Phoenix, I picked up the phone and called Cody Lambert. "Cody, remember when you told me to call you when I got my card? Well, I just got it."

We talked for a couple of minutes about upcoming rodeos. After hanging up with Cody, I made one more call.

"PRCA office," I heard a sweet voice say on the other end of the line. "This is Bea."

"Bea. This is Ty Murray. Have I got some news for you."

4

Pro Rodeo Cowboy

LIVING ON MY OWN and competing with the best in the business was quite an adjustment. I went straight from eating Mom's home cooking and having a curfew on school nights to hitting the road with a bunch of hard-riding, hard-partying cowboys. I held my own, but I had a little learning to do.

One of those lessons came at a college rodeo in Alpine, Texas, a fun town full of classic old West architecture and attitude. It's like going back in a time warp. I rode well that night, and our team put on a great show. But competitive rodeos often continue for hours after the crowds leave the stands. Those events that are staged in front of an audience are considered part of the "performance," and the events that happen after the crowds leave are called the "slack." This night in Alpine, all my riding events were during the performance, but I had to compete in bulldogging in the slack. That meant I had about three hours to kill between my last ride and the bulldogging competition.

"Come on, Ty," Casey Strange, another college cowboy and a good friend of mine, called after the performance was over. "We're going to this bar in town that's supposed to be a blast."

"I can't. I've got to bulldog in the slack."

"Oh, man, that's too bad. I'll tell you what: I'll stay here with you under one condition."

"What's the condition?"

"Come out to my truck and drink beer with me."

That seemed harmless enough. "I'll sit with you for a while," I said. Bulldogging wasn't so tough that I couldn't do it with a few beers in me.

One beer turned into two, which quickly became three, which progressed into four. By the time they got around to the bulldogging competition, I was seeing the world a little fuzzier than before.

Casey said, "Come on, I'll push your steer." There's a barrier in bulldogging that gives the steer a clean and consistent head start. Having somebody push the steer out of the chute is important to timing.

You also have a hazer, somebody to ride along the right side of the steer to keep him moving straight and forward. Riding into the arena, I said to my hazer, "My reflexes are a little slow right now. If you have a better shot than I do, take it." He laughed at the joke, but I was more than a little serious.

The arena at Alpine is huge, and I got out to one of the slowest starts of my career. The steer was well ahead of me as I rode out. I kept closing, but not fast enough. The end of the arena, which was 150 yards from the barrier, a virtual mile in rodeo, kept getting closer and closer, and I kept pushing my horse harder and harder. I knew something had to happen soon or we were going to run out of real estate. Finally, when I got close, I dove for the steer, but I missed. He ran right over the top of me. The breath was knocked out of me, and my shirt had torn completely off my back. My hat was in the dirt, my head was throbbing, and my pride had taken a good licking, all in about fifteen seconds.

I stood up and dusted myself off. Then I heard Casey. He was laughing so hard at the other end of the arena it sounded like somebody had turned a hyena loose. He had tears running down his red face when I got to him. "It's not that funny," I said.

"Oh, hell, yes, it is," he said. Casey swears he still has the remains of the shirt I was wearing that night, although he refuses to produce it for verification.

Needless to say I never drank before another event.

IT DIDN'T TAKE me long to realize that rodeoing and professional rodeoing are worlds apart. Sometimes it's hard to remember that they're the same sport. I'd heard the same thing said about other sports—football and pro football are worlds apart, college basketball and the NBA the same—but I didn't understand what the athletes who said those things were talking about until I experienced it for myself.

For starters, cowboys at the professional rodeo level are more intense than amateurs. In junior rodeos, for example, a select group of us were deadly serious about what we were doing, but some kids rodeoed because their parents thought it was something neat for them to do. In the pros, everybody takes it seriously. Rodeoing is no longer a hobby, a pastime, or a dream; it's how we make our living and feed our families. The arena is our office, and the horses and the bulls are our livelihood.

The second difference I noticed as I was making my professional debut was the talent level. In amateur rodeo, it didn't take long to identify who the top cowboys were on any given night. There might be three or four guys in an event who could really ride, and the rest of the field was a notch or two below them. At the professional level, everybody can ride. The gap in ability from the top cowboy to the twentieth cowboy is so small that most casual observers couldn't tell the difference. That was an adjustment for me. I'd come from a league where I knew the people I needed to beat and what I needed to do to beat them. In the pros, I didn't have that luxury. If you slipped just a little, there was no shortage of guys ready to take your spot away.

Then there is the scheduling, the logistics, the nuances of knowing when to enter a rodeo to get the best stock, coordinating your travel to maximize your time, pacing yourself for a season that can last up to fifty weeks. Every detail, from equipment to meals to car rides to the arena, was now my responsibility. There were no coaches, no front-office managers, no travel secretaries or tour guides to show me how to fly from one rodeo to the next, or how to pack my bronc saddle so it didn't get lost or damaged in the airports, or how to check into a hotel or how to hire a car.

It was a tough adjustment for someone coming straight out of high school or college where parents or coaches handled all the details.

That first year I was blessed to have Cody Lambert as a traveling partner. Before I came along, Cody had been traveling with Tuff Hedeman, Jim Sharp, and Lane Frost, three of the best bull riders in the world. But Cody was also a saddle bronc rider, which made it difficult for him to schedule his travels with Tuff, Jim, and Lane, who only rode bulls. He saw me as the perfect solution. Because I worked multiple events, Cody and I could travel together, share expenses, and not have to worry about conflicting with each other's schedule. It took me a while to realize Cody's motives—he sure didn't talk about them with me—but they made perfect sense.

It also made sense that he should do all the scheduling. He was eight years older than I was, and a seasoned veteran of the rodeo circuit. He knew how and when to book an entry, how and when to travel, where to stay, where to eat, and how to get to the various arenas. I knew nothing. Mom had made all my travel arrangements in amateur rodeo, and my college coach had taken care of all the details at school. I could probably have made a hotel reservation on my own, but that was about it. Plus, having just turned eighteen, I didn't have a credit card, couldn't rent a car, and thought a flight upgrade was when the plane climbed to a higher altitude. Having Cody handle my travel arrangements was a godsend.

I didn't know that he and Dad had worked out an agreement. "Cody," Dad had said. "If Ty runs short of money on the road, you cover it for him and I'll reimburse you." Cody agreed because of his relationship with my family, but neither he nor Dad felt the need to fill me in on it.

On the second day of January, as I prepared to go back to school for the second semester of my freshman year, I made my PRCA debut as an official cardholding cowboy. Fortunately, I didn't have to go far. The opener was in Odessa, only a few miles from campus. It was a nice place to get my feet wet in my first full season as a pro.

I did okay in Odessa, but I drew a tough bull that threw me, and my bareback horse didn't buck enough for much of a score. Sometimes that happens. Because the stock you're going to ride is chosen by a blind draw, at times you get a bull or a bucking horse that's too tough to handle, or one that's too tame to help you rack up points. With half the total score coming from the stock, a good draw can make all the difference.

I had much better luck with my saddle bronc, a good

horse that I scored a 76 on. Cody won the saddle bronc competition that night, and I finished tied for second and took home $453. It wasn't a huge payday, but it was a big deal given what I had in store in the coming weeks.

The next day we left for Denver and one of the biggest and most lucrative rodeos of the year. If I'd had any illusions about waltzing into the PRCA and cherry-picking my events, they were dashed in Denver. I tried to enter all three rough-stock events and didn't get into any of them. The field filled up with the best in the business; rookies need not apply. I stood around and watched as Cody, Tuff, and Jim Sharp all rode. It was tough to be there and watch those guys compete, especially when I felt that I was good enough to be in there with them. But that was the price you paid. In amateur and junior rodeos, I had been The Man. Now I was just another rookie, with not a very good chance of getting into an event like Denver.

Only one thing would change my status in the PRCA. I needed to win. My reputation as a good junior had some weight in the college rodeo ranks, but at the professional level, it didn't matter if I had 1 or 181 amateurs saddles. This was the big league, and I had to prove myself all over again.

We flew from Denver to Portland for our third rodeo in as many weeks. I was still the new kid in our group and the youngest by a fair margin, so I did everything I could to fit in, even when I was catching endless grief from Cody. It started in Denver when we were sharing a hotel room. "Get your ass up!" he shouted in the morning. No nudge or shake or wake-up call. For a minute I thought I was back in the bunkhouse at Larry's ranch and he was about to have me roll out and give him fifty push-ups. But Cody's voice was meaner than Larry's. His patience was a lot thinner as well.

"Bastard" was Cody's most common name for me in those first few months. Sometimes I was a "little bastard," and other times Cody threw in an expletive or two. He never smiled as he said it, and he loved watching me fidget as he chewed my ass out.

Sometimes I deserved a little chiding. When we left for Portland, for example, I had a total of $730 to my name. That included the $453 I'd made in Odessa, along with a little money I had left over from Christmas. I was still a college student, an eighteen-year-old kid, who didn't know how much it cost to travel and who didn't think twice about flying across the country without enough money to get back home. I woke up to the harsh realities of professional rodeo life when American Airlines took $600 of my stash for airfare. Hilton Hotels got the balance, plus another $20. Cody put the hotel room on his credit card, so I was temporarily spared the embarrassment of being short at the check-in counter. But I knew I was broke. If Cody had asked me to pony up right then, I couldn't have done it. Then there were the entry fees. The PRCA didn't float you any credit when it came to entering, and they made it doubly tough on rookies. I couldn't even write a check for my entry fees my first year. In Portland, it wouldn't have mattered since any check I wrote would have bounced. I didn't have enough money to put gas in the rental car.

At dinner our first night in Portland, Cody introduced me to another tradition of the road, one that had my stomach in knots for a few minutes. We were at one of Portland's finer steak houses, where Cody, Jim, Tuff, Lane, and a couple of other bull riders and I had just had one no-holds-barred meal. My first pang of anxiety came when I saw the prices on the menu. In hindsight, the prices were more than reasonable, but at the time anything over a $5 entrée was a new experience for me. I couldn't imagine how a steak could be worth $20, and I had no idea how I was going to pay for it when the bill finally came. The rest of the guys ordered appetizers, salads, drinks, and sides. A couple of them even had dessert. When the bill came, I didn't look at it, but a top-of-my-head calculation put it at around $500.

"Okay, who's going to pick the number?" Cody asked.

"What number?" I asked. I didn't know what he was talking about.

"Stupid little bastard," Cody said.

Jim Sharp filled me in: "Whenever we go out like this, we play a numbers game to see who picks up the check. Somebody writes down a number on a napkin, and we go around the table guessing. The person who guesses the closest number to the one on the napkin pays the bill. The person who wrote the number down takes one number higher than the one picked by the guy on his right. It's a pretty fun game, and if you do it all year, it evens out."

Evening out at year's end was the last thing on my mind. I didn't have enough money to pay the bar tab, and we were choosing numbers to take care of the whole bill!

I didn't have it, didn't have any way of getting it, and if I had lost, I either would have had to beg Cody to bail me out, or I would have been washing dishes for the rest of the weekend. The odds were in my favor, but I still had a one-in-six chance of being in deep trouble.

I don't remember what number I picked, nor do I recall if anybody noticed the sweat that broke out on my forehead, but I played. Fortunately I didn't lose that night, and I was able to compete in Portland without anybody knowing how broke I was.

Those worries were over a day later when I rode a Western Trails Rodeo Company bronc for 79 points and won the saddle bronc event in Portland. I'd only gotten into two of the first three rodeos of the year, but I'd finished second in the bronc riding in one and won the bronc riding in the other. That gave me the early lead in the bonus pools like the Coors Chute Out and Dodge Truck Series. It also put me in the all-around lead for Rookie of the Year. After that week in Portland, I never worried about money again, and my dad never had to reimburse Cody a dime.

Even though I was winning, I still had my fair share of first-year troubles, the first being my inability to get up in the morning. Contrary to what some people might think, not all cowboys get up with the chickens. Most rodeos are held at night, which means a lot of rodeo cowboys don't get out of the arena until well after midnight. At times I would go weeks without hitting the pillow until one or two in the morning. That makes it tough to get up and out at a time most people would call reasonable.

Cody was a naturally early riser, which worked out perfectly for us. He made all the travel arrangements and entered all the rodeos, so the quiet morning hours were a perfect time for him to get organized. But when he was ready for me to get up, he wanted me up right then. I couldn't hit the snooze button or put a pillow over my head. When Cody woke me up, I was supposed to get up and get moving. Being eighteen, I wasn't much of a morning person. Just like when I was staying with Larry Mahan, I loved my sleep, and I liked taking a little extra time getting upright.

"Get your ass up, now!" Cody would shout. Finally, he came in one morning and said, "I've had it. From this moment on I'm telling you one time to get your sorry, lazy ass out of the bed. If you don't get up, I'm not telling you again. I'm leaving you. I don't care where we are or what we're supposed to be doing, if you're not up, your ass is left."

I never overslept again.

Cody and I complemented each other, but it was tough for both of us that first year. He was already married with a child, and I was a kid less than a year removed from having a curfew and a bedtime. I used to hear him tell people, "I feel like I've got two kids now," when my name came up. At the time I was hurt and a little angered by those comments, but in hindsight I realize he was right. The eighteen-year-old me would have driven the twenty-six-year-old me crazy. I had to have been a nightmare to Cody.

At least the sleep issue wasn't a problem anymore. I knew he meant what he said about leaving me. From that point forward I was a one "get your ass up" guy. All he had to do was call me.

This was evidenced a little later in the year at a rodeo in Salinas, California. The weekend had gone pretty well. I'd had some good draws and some good rides, including what I thought was a good bull ride. I was preparing to step off my bull after riding him pretty well. But a ride is never over until you're on the ground and safely out of the way of the bull. As my leg was coming over the top of the bull, my spur hung in my rope just long enough to whip me down and knock me unconscious. The last thing I remember thinking was "Man, this is going to hurt."

Cody made his way to where I was lying. "Get your ass up, now!" he shouted. I don't remember it, but those in attendance that day say that I shot straight up. Cody's tough conditioning had obviously worked.

Looking back, I realize how lost I would have been without Cody. Entering rodeos is as much of an art as it is a science, and nobody was better than Cody at visualizing where we needed to be and how we needed to get there. In addition to knowing what rodeos had the best stock and the best purses, he knew which towns had easy airport access, what days the best stock was going to be out, and what the travel times were between events so we could double up and enter two or three different rodeos in a single weekend. During one Fourth of July week—Cowboy Christmas as it's called, the busiest seven days of the year for a rodeo cowboy—we competed in eleven different rodeos in eleven different cities in nine days. These weren't next-door cities either. During that week we rode in Pecos, Texas; St. Paul, Oregon; Molalla, Oregon; Eugene, Oregon; Ponoka, Alberta; Calgary, Alberta; Prescott, Arizona; Window Rock, Arizona; Cody, Wyoming; Greeley, Colorado; and Springdale, Arkansas.

Cody tried to enter the events so that we were never scheduled to be at two places at the same time. Computers decided when you rode, so you never had full control over your schedule. But Cody was a master at maximizing our time. He chartered airplanes and lined up ground transportation so that the minute we finished at one place, we could hop in the car, rush to the airport, get on a plane, fly to the next city, hop in another car, and make it to the arena in time to loosen up and make another ride. Without him, I would have been lost. Here I was a kid who'd never flown on a commercial airplane until I was in college. Suddenly I was winning rodeos, collecting checks every week, making more money than I could count, and traveling in chartered airplanes and rented cars. It was a huge jump, one I could never have made on my own. I could barely keep up with all the money I was making.

One week I rode in Calgary, then flew immediately back to Texas for an exhibition and some much needed downtime at home. I won the Calgary rodeo, but hadn't hung around to pick up my check, so Jim Sharp collected it for me. But Jim didn't come straight back to Texas. He went to California for a week, then to Arizona, before finally hooking up with me three weeks later.

When I finally saw him again, Jim handed me a check for $8,000 and said, "There's your money."

"What's that for?" I asked.

"Calgary. You didn't hang around to collect your check."

"Thanks. I'd forgotten about it."

That's the way we lived those early years. Cody, Jim, Lane Frost, Tuff Hedeman, and I were as close as brothers. We fought like family and looked after one another like siblings. We'd ride together, eat together, bunk together, split expenses, and encourage each other every week. Cody was the elder statesman of our bunch, and he never let any of us forget it. He'd chew all our asses out at the drop of a hat, but in the next breath he'd defend us to the death.

Lane Frost was the politician, and the best-looking guy in our group. He had a smile that could break up a fight, and he probably signed more autographs than the rest of us combined.

Tuff Hedeman was a quiet hard-ass, a guy who could cut you with his gaze and who didn't take crap off anybody. He and Lane had traveled together for years, bunking in the backseats of cars and eating junk food from cheap gas stations before either of them had much success. Now they were flying and staying in hotels with the rest of us.

Jim Sharp was the coolest customer in our group. The winner of two consecutive national college rodeo championships in bull riding, Jim had earned the respect of the older guys by finishing fourth in the world in bull riding in his rookie year and taking Rookie of the Year honors by a mile. But no matter how good or how bad he rode, he was always the same cool guy. We used to joke that Jim was the only guy who could come back into the locker room after a ride and nobody could tell if he'd won or gotten thrown off.

During one of our road trips together, Jim and I were in the backseat while Cody and Lane rode up front. "Man, that Tyson fight is going to be good this weekend," Lane said.

"Yeah," Cody said. "That boy's as bad as I've ever seen. I don't think anybody can touch him."

After a second or two of silence Jim said, "I'm going to see it."

"You're going to the fight?" Lane asked.

"Yep."

"You're going to Atlantic City this weekend?" Cody said.

"Atlantic City?" Jim said. "I thought it was at the Odessa Coliseum."

After bursting a gut laughing, Cody said, "You damned idiot, that's a closed-circuit telecast they're showing in there. The fight's in Atlantic City. You're paying to watch the damn thing on a movie screen."

"Aw, man, I thought they were fighting in Odessa."

We all got a big laugh out of that one, and Jim was laughing right along with us. That was one of the reasons he was no fun to pick on: he'd laugh at himself harder than you could laugh at him. Fans nicknamed him "Razor" Jim Sharp, which I always thought was funny. Jim was duller than a rusty bed knife. The only thing razor sharp about him was his riding, which was second to none.

I was the kid of the bunch, younger, smaller, quieter, and greener. Thankfully, I had those guys to take care of me. There's no telling what would have happened if I'd hit the road on my own.

The first time in my entire career I attempted to coordinate and travel to multiple rodeos on my own, it turned out to be the worst mistake I'd ever made, and the longest three days of my life.

IT SHOULD HAVE been easy. Two rodeos in one weekend was nothing unusual for professional cowboys. Sometimes we rode in three or four different rodeos in one three-day period. This time I made the arrangements myself. I entered one event in Swift Current, Saskatchewan, Canada, and another in St. George, Utah. I had the thing timed out perfectly. I'd ride on Friday in Canada, Saturday in Utah, and Sunday again in Swift Current. The private plane was lined up, the car was rented, the hotels were booked, and I had Marvin Garrett, a world champion bareback rider, and his brother Mark, making the trip with me to split expenses. What could possibly go wrong?

The commercial flight from Dallas to Calgary went smoothly, but that's where my good fortune ended. At the rental-car counter a smiling attendant in a bright green uniform informed me that my MasterCard had been denied. "It what?" I said.

"Your card has been denied. Do you have another credit card?"

By that time in my career I had plenty of cards and plenty of cash, but this was the only one I'd brought with me for this trip. After the shock wore off, I realized I had a $7,000 credit limit on that card, and the hotels, chartered plane, and airline ticket to Calgary had bumped me up against the limit. I called MasterCard and pleaded my case: "I have plenty of money. Just look at my credit history. You guys need to extend my credit on this card so I can rent a car."

"We'll have to get back to you," the customer service rep said.

"You need to hurry. I've got a five-hour drive from Calgary to Swift Current, Saskatchewan, and the rodeo starts in six hours."

"I'll see what we can do," he said in a tone that didn't give me much hope.

An hour later with panic setting in, I started calling every cowboy I knew: "Hey, I'm stuck in Calgary and the rodeo starts in five hours." Most of the guys I reached were already in Swift Current. "You've got a problem," most of them said.

At 2:35 P.M., three hours and twenty-five minutes before the rodeo was to start, I finally got a call from MasterCard. "Mr. Murray, you're such a good customer, we'd be happy to extend your line of credit," the chipper woman on the end of the line said.

"Good. Just do it right now. I'm already late."

This time, the card was approved. I had three hours to make a five-hour drive, find the rodeo, park, check in, put on my pads, spurs, tape, and bareback rigging, then stretch before riding. Something was going to have to give.

"Would you like the collision insurance, Mr. Murray?" the cheerful agent asked.

"No, decline everything. Just give me a car, quick."

The dot matrix printer took forever to print out my rental agreement. "What kind of car would you like, sir?"

"I want the fastest one you've got on the lot."

That turned out to be a Buick LeSabre with a V-8. I threw my bronc saddle and rigging bag into the backseat, fired the LeSabre up, and floored it. The tires squealed as I fishtailed out of the parking lot. Fortunately the expressway was near the airport. By the time I merged onto the four-lane, the car had topped 100 mph.

Although I've never spoken to a GM engineer about it, I have discovered that Buicks are redline governed. When your rpm exceed the maximum, the engine slows. For the V-8 LeSabre, that feature kicks in at about 116 miles per hour, which is the speed I maintained from the moment I left the Calgary airport until I arrived in Swift Current. Along the way I passed cars, trucks, vans, and RVs on the left, right, and both shoulders. For three straight hours I kept that car going as fast as the engine would allow. I got a sense of what race-car drivers must experience.

By some miracle of modern automotive technology, I

drove 310 miles from Calgary to Swift Current in just under three hours. By then the speed was getting good to me. I felt like I owned the road. The one thing I didn't anticipate was how long it took to slow down.

I hit the Swift Current exit ramp at over 100 mph. Before I knew it, the stop sign at the end of the ramp was on me, and I was nowhere close to being stopped. I hit the brakes and slid sideways through the intersection. If anything had been coming in either direction, I would have been toast.

By the grace of God, I was the only person on the road, so I spun the tires again and ripped it up the side street. If I hurried, I might make it to the rodeo before my name was called. It took me a couple of seconds to realize I was going the wrong way. No problem. There was a side street just ahead. Two quick lefts, and I should be back on track.

I saw the Wrong Way: Do Not Enter sign long after I had committed to the turn and punched the throttle. Now I was going the wrong way on a one-way street with no idea how to get to the rodeo.

Not that it mattered. I checked my mirror to see if I could turn around, and the blue lights pierced the rear window like a laser. After three hours of 116 mph driving, I was being stopped for making an illegal turn. I didn't see the two other patrol cars until I was completely stopped. One in front, one in back, and one angled at my side; this was not a good sign. When the cops drew their weapons and shielded themselves behind their car doors, I realized the gravity of my situation.

"He's going to jail," one of the officers said after I explained myself. The driver of one of the vehicles I had blown past had phoned the police. They knew I was coming and were waiting for me. Not only had these cops seen me barreling down the expressway at over 100 mph, they'd seen me miss the stop sign, slide through the intersection, and fishtail the wrong way up a one-way street. At that moment I had to agree with the officer's assessment. I was going to jail.

"You're Ty Murray, aren't you?" one of the cops asked me before seeing my ID. This was a good sign. By this stage in my career my face had appeared on several advertisements and on the covers of a few magazines. I wasn't as recognizable as Michael Jordan or Tiger Woods, but rodeo fans knew me on sight. That meant this cop was probably a rodeo fan.

"Yeah," I said. "I was on my way to the Swift Current rodeo, but . . ."

"Let me take him," the cop said.

"No way," another said. "He's going in."

There were huddles and high-strung negotiations behind one of the police cars. When they broke and came back to where I was standing, my cop said, "Okay, you're coming with me." The other cops weren't happy, but they begrudgingly got in their cars and left. "Now, here's what we're going to do. I'm going to take you to this rodeo, where you are going to ride. The moment you finish, you are going to call me—not the station house, not the dispatcher—me. I'm allowing you to ride, but then I'm taking you to see the judge."

I couldn't agree fast enough. By this time it was 6:05.

The rodeo was under way and I was nowhere near ready. I threw my bronc saddle in the back of the patrol car, and we took off, sirens blaring, toward the rodeo.

Every eye in the place was on us as we cruised through security and past all the rigs. We stopped right behind the chutes with the blue lights flashing. I jumped out just in time to put on my spurs and make my first ride.

I competed in all three roughstock events that night and did reasonably well, given the circumstances. When I finished, I immediately called my new best friend, the officer whose name I never got. Within minutes he was back at the rodeo. I loaded my gear back into his car, and we rode off to Saskatchewan night court.

At first the judge looked like he was going to throw the book at me. But my cop friend did everything in his power to paint a rosy picture of what I'd done: "Mr. Murray was very cooperative. Road conditions were clear, and traffic was light. No one was immediately threatened by Mr. Murray's actions."

After scowling at me from the bench for fifteen minutes, the judge said, "Mr. Murray, the normal punishment for this offense is a thousand-dollar fine and year's suspension of your license. Because of your cooperation, your attitude, your obvious contrition, and the endorsement of the arresting officer, I'm going to fine you five hundred dollars and suspend your license for six months."

I didn't care if they suspended my license forever. It was Canada. If I never drove up here again, it would be fine.

"Thank you, Your Honor," I said. Then I reached into my bag and pulled out my checkbook.

"What's that?" the judge said.

"It's my checkbook."

"Sorry. We don't take checks. It's cash only."

At the time I had about $50 in my pocket, a development that left the judge shrugging his shoulders and raising his eyebrows, the universal sign for "not my problem." It looked as though I was going to jail after all.

Then my newest and dearest best friend piped up, "Is there somewhere you can get the money?"

"Yeah," I said. "If I can get back to the sponsoring hotel, I can get it."

"Your Honor, if it pleases the court, I will escort Mr. Murray to a nearby hotel where he can acquire the necessary funds to pay his fine, and we can dismiss this matter."

"Fine," the judge said, pointing his finger at the cop. "But he's your responsibility."

By the time we got to the sponsoring hotel, my arresting officer had been off duty for hours. He was simply helping me out. As is always the case after a rodeo, I found a number of contract hands and industry reps in the hotel lounge, along with a few cowboys who were having a late dinner. Armed with a napkin and a pen, I set out asking everyone, "Have you got any money you can let me borrow?" I kept notes of those who contributed to the Get Ty Out of Jail Fund—Ben gave $50; J.W. gave $90; Ronny gave $10—until I had finally collected the $500. By the time I paid the fine, got fingerprinted, photographed, signed the necessary paperwork, and hitched a ride back to the hotel, it was well past 3 A.M. And my weekend had just started.

I WAS SURPRISED by how good I felt the next morning. Despite my brush with the law, I had ridden well in the rodeo and stood a good chance of winning at least one, and maybe two, events in the short round, which concluded on Sunday. In the meantime, I had to fly to St. George, Utah, with Marvin and Mark Garrett. This was a special one-day rodeo. Only the top riders were competing. It was a great honor to be invited. Of course, to compete, we had to get there first.

The plane, a twin-prop Beechcraft, took off on time with me in the copilot's seat, and Marvin and Mark in the back. The hum of the engines and the steady vibration of the ride had me nodding off minutes after takeoff. I was asleep before the landing gear was up. I don't know how long I was out before the pilot punched my shoulder, but it couldn't have been long. "What?" I asked.

"We're not going to make it."

This is not the kind of thing anyone likes to hear in an airplane. It ranks up there with "Hold on" and "It's been an honor flying with you" as one of those phrases you'd be happy to go your whole life without hearing. "What do you mean we're not going to make it?" The sky looked clear. I could still hear the engines. We weren't losing altitude, at least not that I could tell.

"I mean we're not going to get there in time," the pilot said. "We've got a head wind of over a hundred knots. We're not going to make it to St. George in time."

I looked down and saw what he meant. It looked like cars on the interstates below us were going faster. "What's the nearest airport?"

"Riverton, Wyoming."

"Okay, land in Riverton." I didn't have a plan, but I knew we weren't going to make it in this plane. On the ground at least I could try to make other arrangements.

Once we were on the ground, I jumped out of the plane and called Steve Gilbert, the promoter of the St. George rodeo. "Steve, this is Ty Murray. I'm stuck in Riverton, Wyoming, with Marvin and Mark Garrett. We've got a hundred-knot head wind, and our plane is not going to make it."

"Don't move," Steve said. "I'll have a Learjet there in twenty minutes."

Nineteen minutes and fifty seconds later, a black Lear 35 taxied to the FBO where the three of us were sitting. Five minutes after that we were soaring toward Utah, late again. When we landed, Marvin looked out the window and said, "I ain't believing this." I looked out and saw three Utah State Patrol cars waiting for us on the tarmac. For the second time in two days, I rode to the rodeo in a police car and was dropped off behind the chutes with the blue lights flashing.

It was another successful night at the rodeo. I rode well and made a decent amount of money. Afterward I checked into a local hotel, ate a great meal, and crashed, sleeping harder than I can remember sleeping in a long time. Sunday it was back to Swift Current for the short round. I just hoped that day would go smoother than the rest of the weekend.

This turned out to be wishful thinking. Our pilot waited on us in Riverton, Wyoming, because Steve Gilbert volunteered his Learjet and pilots for the jaunt back across the state line. By the time we had loaded everything back in the small Beechcraft, I felt that things were moving in the right direction. We'd had a huge head wind on the way down from Swift Current, so I figured we'd have a great tailwind on the way back.

Thunderstorms never entered my mind.

Just as had happened the day before, the throaty rumble of the piston engines lulled all three of us to sleep. Only this time when the pilot punched me in the shoulder, I knew it wasn't good news. "You're not going to believe this, but we're not going to make it."

"You have got to be kidding me." When I opened my eyes, I saw that he wasn't. The sky looked like black death in front of us. It was the biggest, blackest thunderstorm I had ever seen, and we were heading straight toward it.

"I could go around it," the pilot said, "but it would take all day. You'd miss the rodeo."

"Turn around and head back to Riverton." This time I had a plan. If those two Learjet pilots were still around, I thought we would hire them to fly us back to Canada. To my surprise (given how our luck had run all weekend), the black jet was still on the tarmac.

The pilots hadn't flown back to Utah. They were out having breakfast at a nearby diner. Once again, three champion cowboys sat our butts on the bench outside the Riverton FBO and waited on a ride.

I had pulled my hat down over my eyes when I heard a voice say, "What are you guys doing here?" It was one of the pilots.

"You're back!" I said. "Listen, we hit a monster thunderstorm on our way back north. Can we hire you to fly us back to Swift Current?"

"Sure," the second pilot said as he came out of the FBO with a cup of coffee in his hand. "The only problem is, you'll have to clear customs in Calgary."

This was when I could have kicked myself. I had cleared Canadian customs on my first trip into Calgary on Friday, the day of my high-speed reckless-driving arrest, which seemed like an eternity ago. It had never occurred to me that flying to Utah and attempting to enter Canada again by private plane would cause a problem. "Why Calgary?" I asked.

"It's Sunday," the pilot said. "There are only a couple of places you can clear on a Sunday, and Calgary's the closest."

We were barely going to make it on time as it was. A detour to Calgary would cause us to miss the event altogether. "Let me see what I can do," I said, as if I knew where to start when it came to international customs problems. With nowhere else to turn, I called the rodeo office in Swift Current. After being transferred around a few times, I finally got the rodeo promoter on the line. "We've got a problem," I said. After explaining our customs situation, the rodeo promoter, whose name I didn't know then and don't know to this day, said he would make a few calls and get back to me. Ten minutes later the phone rang.

"I've spoken with the customs office, and they've agreed to clear you through by phone once you land in Swift Current," he said. "Someone will be waiting on the phone when you arrive."

When I hung up, I shouted, "I got it!" and within five minutes we were airborne.

I almost fell asleep again, but I knew it would be a bad omen to close my eyes. Instead I looked out the window and thought about how much work and effort had gone into this one two-rodeo weekend. I wondered if this was the kind of stuff Cody had to deal with every week. If it was, I didn't know how he kept his sanity. At least it was almost over, I told myself.

"Hey!" the pilot yelled, pointing his finger in my direction. "Did you lie to me?"

"Lie to you about what?"

He motioned to his headset. "They're asking us why we're vectoring to Swift Current without clearing customs in Calgary."

"No. We got permission."

"Permission from whom?"

That was the problem. Saying "the rodeo promoter" sounded lame, even to me. The situation was compounded by the fact that I didn't know the promoter's name.

"You lied to me!" the pilot shouted.

"No, no. The guy at the rodeo said he'd cleared it. They were going to clear us over the phone."

"Yeah, right," the pilot said to me before relaying the message.

We flew around in circles over the Swift Current airport for another fifteen minutes until someone finally radioed back and told the pilots that we did, indeed, have clearance to land in Swift Current, and that we would, indeed, be cleared through customs over the phone.

Late, tired, and punch-drunk from three days in travel purgatory, I had one of the best riding days of my year, winning the bull riding and finishing second in the bronc riding in the short round at Swift Current, while Marvin went on to win the bareback riding event. It was the perfect ending to an awful weekend, one I'll never forget, and one I vowed never to repeat. From that moment forward, I swore that no matter what I had to do—pay him, wash his truck, beg him, call him *jefe* for the rest of his life—I was getting Cody Lambert to handle my scheduling for the rest of my rodeo career.

• • •

I HAVE NO IDEA how many pitfalls Cody saved me from during my rookie season. He sure didn't tell me. At times I thought he kept me around so he'd have somebody to pick on at all times. One week, when his wife came to watch us compete, Cody wanted to give her some checks to take home and deposit. "Ty," he said. "You need to give me three thousand dollars."

"What for?"

"What the hell do you mean, 'What for?' You idiot. Who do you think paid your entry fees, hotel rooms, and plane fares for the past month? You owe me three thousand and I need to make a deposit."

"Okay." I fished around in my bag for my address book. When I found my book, I opened it and rummaged through all the uncashed checks I had from rodeos throughout the year. A $300 check here, an $1,100 check there, and pretty soon I had close to the exact amount I owed him.

"What . . ." Cody's eyes got big as he reached for my address book. "What the hell do you have in there?" When he saw the stack of uncashed checks, totaling close to $40,000, he went ballistic. "You ignorant little bastard! Have you never heard of a bank? This is like carrying a suitcase full of cash everywhere you go. If you lost that book, you'd lose forty thousand dollars. You ignorant, stupid little bastard."

He was right, of course. At age eighteen I only thought about the money as a way of measuring how I stood compared to the rest of the competition. As long as I had a bed to sleep in, good food to eat, and a rodeo to enter, I was happy. Cashing my winnings wasn't a priority. What would I have done with all that money anyway? Plus, I enjoyed the competitive aspects of winning money more than the money itself. During one plane ride from Phoenix to Houston, Cody, Tuff, Jim, and I struck up a high-stakes poker game. I had less card-playing experience than any of those guys, but I still came out the big winner. At the end of the weekend I couldn't wait to call home: "Dad, we got in a poker game on the plane and I won three thousand dollars."

Dad said, "Well, how'd you do in the rodeo?"

"Oh, yeah. I won that too. I made forty-five hundred there."

I CAN'T SAY that my riding improved considerably my rookie year, but I certainly matured, both physically and mentally. In the spring, just before the busiest time of the year, my right hand began to swell. It started as an annoyance, but as the spring wore on and we were riding every day, the pain kept getting worse. Finally I asked Cody what he thought it was. "Your bareback rigging is too small for your hand," he said.

"How's that possible?"

"You little bastard, you've grown. The good news is, all you have to do is get a bigger rigging. The bad news is, your hand's already messed up and we're entering the busiest part of the year. It's going to be sore all summer, so get used to it."

He was right on all counts. I had outgrown my rigging without realizing it. A simple change in equipment was all I needed to correct the problem. But the damage was done. My hand would give me problems the rest of my rookie year.

I had also outgrown my bronc saddle because my legs were longer than they had been when I'd first started out. I got a new saddle, and the stirrups were a little long. Once again, Cody was there to validate my decision when I said, "I think I'm going to take my stirrups up a little bit."

"Damn, I'm glad to hear you say that. I've been thinking that same thing every night."

"Well, why didn't you say something?"

"You didn't ask. You've always thought I rode with mine too short, so I wasn't going to jump in there and coach you. I figured if you needed help, you'd ask."

This was one of the unwritten rules of professional rodeo that I learned in my rookie season. Cowboys are more than happy to help each other, but you never offer unsolicited advice. I learned pretty quickly that if I needed help or wanted some advice, all I had to do was ask. But unlike my junior days when Dad and I would critique every ride, as a pro, if I didn't ask for help, nobody was going to offer an opinion.

As the season wore on and Cody and I passed the one hundred rodeos mark for the year, my body began to show the effects of being a rookie. I had a torn calf muscle, my hand was so swollen it looked like I'd stuck it in a hornets' nest, I had dislocated one of my toes, and every part of my body was sore. The increased schedule was the biggest adjustment I'd had to make. As a junior and an amateur I would ride three times a week. As a pro, I was riding every day in addition to traveling and repairing my own equipment. Sure, I was young, but my body hadn't adjusted to the rigors of a pro rodeo schedule.

As my pain and fatigue mounted, my riding fell off. At the Calgary Stampede, a bull called First Blood pitched me headfirst into the dirt. Those sorts of wrecks are never much fun, but this one hurt worse than normal. The dirt in the arena was compacted and I was thrown pretty hard. Plus I was tired and sore to begin with, so getting a faceful of dirt stung worse than normal. Then I missed a number of bareback rides when my hand got too sore to ride. By the time we went to Deadwood, South Dakota, in the fall, I was whipped. I needed some rest.

"Why don't you go home and rest, you little puss," Cody said. "Are you tired? Are you sore? You want to run home to Mama? That's fine. I've worn out a lot a little weak-hearts in my day. If you can't cut it, head on home."

I told him I was fine. I could gut it out. Playing hurt was part of the game, but that didn't stop me from thinking, "This guy's trying to kill me." Plus I was leading the rookie standings, and I didn't want to miss any rodeos for fear of falling behind in the Rookie of the Year race. Still, I wasn't sure how much good I was doing myself staying out on the road in this condition.

Later that weekend Cody found my uncle Butch Myers at the rodeo in Deadwood. "Hey, Butch," he said. "You really need to talk Ty into going home and getting some rest. He's worn-out, and he's not doing himself any good staying out here."

That was the way Cody operated. To my face he would be the meanest, toughest SOB I'd ever been around. Then he'd go behind my back and have my uncle tell me to go home and get some rest. Or he'd have another cowboy tell me that my bull rope wasn't the most modern thing in the world and I should consider upgrading. These were all things Cody knew, but he would have others tell me. That was his nature. And it's part of why he remains my best friend in the world to this day.

ONE OF THE MOST valuable lessons I learned from Cody during my rookie season was the benefit of spending a little more money to travel first-class. From the moment we started out together, we flew from city to city, stayed in nice hotels located near the rodeos, and ate good meals in nice restaurants. Sure it cost more. But when I looked at the cowboys who drove across the country to every event, who slept in their trucks, or who crammed eight guys into a cheap motel room with fast-food wrappers scattered all over the floor, I knew we had made the right choice. Not only were we fresher and more focused when it came time to ride, we didn't dread the travel nearly as much as some other guys, even after 111 rodeos and a lot of bumps and bruises.

Some folks thought that somehow went against the spirit of what it meant to be a cowboy; that, to be a real cowboy, you had to ride around busted flat, live out of your car, eat Twinkies, and hope to make enough for gas money to the next rodeo. Flying first-class and eating in nice restaurants somehow wasn't the cowboy way in their eyes. I thought that was crazy. Cody had traveled that way before. When Tuff, Lane, and Cody had first hit the road, they used to sleep three to a bed in the cheapest fleabag motels they could find, driving across the country in an old car that leaked oil and was in constant need of new shocks.

Maybe that was romantic in some people's eyes, but I thought it sucked, and Cody agreed. If we were going to go out on the road, we were at least going to travel as comfortably as possible. That didn't make me any less a cowboy. I still wore my hat at the dinner table and I went out carousing with the boys, but it didn't mean I had to travel like a vagabond.

Being fresher, well rested, better fed, and more focused also allowed me to comfortably enter all three roughstock events consistently, something few cowboys chose to do. Sometimes I heard other people say things like "It's just too expensive to enter all three events." That never made sense to me. If I was at a rodeo, the travel expenses, the hotel room, and my meals were going to be the same whether I entered one event or three. The only added expense was my entry fee, which I saw as an investment, not an expense. The more events I entered, the more chances I had to earn a check.

By year's end, that strategy had paid off. Even though I had injured my hand and missed a good number of bareback events in my rookie season, I still won the PRCA Rookie of the Year award. Saddle bronc riding, the event that had been my weakest only four years before, was my strongest event in my rookie season. I earned $24,391 in saddle bronc events in 1988, which put me twenty-fifth in the world and second to Craig Latham in the rookie standings. Then I won $14,119 in bull riding, finishing second in rookie earnings to David Berry, who won $14,306. In bareback riding, I only won $7,467, but that was $1,100 more than any other rookie bareback rider won all year. My combined earnings were $45,977; not bad for a college freshman who had just turned nineteen.

At the National Finals Rodeo in 1988, I rode into the center of the arena at the Thomas and Mack Center in a Binion's stagecoach. With great fanfare, the MC presented me with a Rookie of the Year belt buckle, a hat, and an oversize cardboard check for $2,000. I was thrilled, but I was also a little disappointed. Winning the Rookie of the Year title had been my goal and I couldn't have been happier to win it, but I had also wanted to qualify for the NFR. The PRCA national championship (the National Finals Rodeo, or NFR) only accepts the top fifteen earners in each category. While I'd been close in all three roughstock events, I hadn't quite made it into the top fifteen in any of them.

Having to watch my sport's ultimate event as a spectator was disappointing. It was also motivating. As I looked around the arena and waved to the fans who were applauding my Rookie of the Year award, I knew I would be back. "Next time," I said to myself, "I won't be watching from the stands."

5

First Buckle

IN OUR SPORT, you go from being a kid to a man real quick. By the time my second year rolled around, I felt like a seasoned veteran, even though I was only nineteen and a sophomore in college. I had missed the NFR my first year, but won the Rookie of the Year title in both the PRCA and in the National Intercollegiate Rodeo Association. It wasn't everything I'd hoped it would be, but it was a solid start.

Balancing school and rodeoing was tough, especially in the winter and spring when I was rodeoing both for Odessa College and in as many PRCA events as I could enter. When I'd signed with Odessa, I'd told my coach, Jim Watkins, "I promise you I'll be here two years. You won't ever have to worry about my grades. I won't ever miss a college rodeo no matter what's going on in the PRCA. And I plan on winning a national college championship for you."

So far, I'd kept my word. I consistently made the dean's

list, and because my teachers could see that I was willing to go the extra mile to make up work and keep them apprised of my travels, they went out of their way to help me. Cowboys had never been known for their academic prowess—bucking stock and bailing hay usually took precedent over Copernicus and John Maynard Keynes—so I think my teachers went way out of their way when they saw that I had classroom potential.

I never missed a college rodeo, either, even going so far as to hire a local dentist to fly me in his private plane from a PRCA event back to Odessa. I had my share of fun, but I hadn't had any major problems my freshman year—no suspensions or reprimands, which often befall first-year students—and I entered my second year of school with a great deal of confidence. The only promise I hadn't kept so far was winning a college national title. That became Goal Number One for 1989.

As a second-year student I moved out of the dorm and into an apartment with Jim Sharp, who lived in Odessa when he wasn't on the road. Jim was only two years my senior, but he had already won a world bull riding title and was considered one of the greats of the sport. He was one of the guys I had looked up to when I was coming through the junior ranks; not quite a contemporary, but close enough in age that I could be motivated by his accomplishments.

He was also the guy I was supposed to replace at Odessa. Coach Watkins had recruited me in the hope that I could take Jim's place when he graduated. They were big shoes to fill, but

I felt I was up to the task. Now, Jim and I were living to-gether. He had gone from being one of my heroes to somebody I competed against week in and week out. I still admired his skills, and his stable, never-rattled demeanor was something I would try to emulate throughout my entire career.

He was like a Clint Eastwood character, cool, calm, and deadly when he needed to be. At the 1988 NFR, he stood a chance to be the first man in history to ride all ten bulls without being thrown in a single round. With each passing round, the pressure intensified. Lane Frost had made it nine rounds the year he won the world title, but an awful rank bull named Red Rock threw him in the tenth. Jim made it through nine rounds without any trouble.

For most guys that sort of situation would be pressure-packed. It's like a starting pitcher taking a perfect game into the ninth inning. As the tenth round of riding got under way, the crowd, the judges, even the other riders, were on edge about possibly seeing something nobody had ever seen. But when I came upon Jim sitting on the floor of the tunnel lead-ing from the locker room to the arena, he was eating a hot dog and drinking a Coke like a spectator. "What the hell are you doing?" I said.

"I'm eating a dog. What the hell does it look like?" he said.

I just shook my head and walked off. That was Jim, through and through. Not thirty minutes later he was in the arena making history by becoming the first cowboy ever to ride all ten of his bulls in the NFR.

The crowd went nuts! They'd just seen a perfect game, an undefeated season, and a world record all rolled into one. Jim just did what he always did: tipped his hat and nodded to the crowd before sauntering back to the locker room.

We had become great friends during my rookie year. Now, we were roommates.

We lived on the second floor of an old West saddle shop, a clapboard building that looked like something straight out of the 1800s. Half of the downstairs had been designated for storage, so we converted that area into a gym with free weights, dumbbells, and a bench. Jim and I would work out every day, no matter what we'd done or how late we'd stayed out the night before. We had made a pact with each other: sticking to that rule kept me in check when my teenage instincts were screaming for me to enjoy the party a little more.

Not that we didn't have a good time at our apartment. After the first few months of the fall semester, our place earned the nickname the Bronco House. We kept it pretty Western, and there weren't many times our guests left unhappy. We were young cowboys, richer than we'd ever been in our lives, out on our own and living our dreams. We thought we were studs.

We certainly weren't idle. My first trip of the new season came right at the end of the old year. The 1989 Texas Circuit Finals Rodeo was held during the Christmas holidays, from December 28 through the thirty-first. After downing a little turkey and opening presents with the family, I headed to the Northside Coliseum in Fort Worth for my first event as reigning Rookie of the Year.

Not that the title meant anything—the bulls and bucking horses couldn't have cared less that I was wearing a Rookie of the Year buckle—but performing at the level I did in 1988 made me a little more comfortable with the other aspects of the PRCA circuit. I wasn't the kid who didn't know which end was up anymore, or the plebe every veteran cowboy picked on. Cody was still tough on me, but even he'd backed off a little. I wasn't the "little bastard" or the "puss" anymore. Now we were just veteran cowboys, traveling partners, and best friends.

I got off to a great start in Fort Worth, winning the saddle bronc title and finishing second in the bareback event for a total take of $4,062. That was good enough to capture the all-around title and earn a spot in the prestigious Dodge National Circuit Finals Rodeo to be held in Pocatello, Idaho, in March. The title was great, but just as important to me was whom I beat to win it. This was a big rodeo, one of the ones I would have had a hard time getting into in my rookie year. To win the saddle bronc title I had to beat Dave Appleton, the reigning PRCA world all-around champion cowboy. Dave wore the buckle I wanted, the one Larry Mahan had captured six times. To beat Dave in his bread-and-butter event was a big boost to my confidence.

That confidence carried over throughout the spring in both college rodeos and the PRCA. I rode bareback and saddle broncs better than I ever had. Unfortunately, I had some tough draws and some bad luck in bull riding, which got me off to a slow start. But this was where competing in all three roughstock events helped me. If I had been only a bull rider, or a cowboy who primarily rode bulls and occasionally competed on saddle broncs, I would never have led the rankings in 1989, because bull riding was my weakest event that year. This wasn't entirely my fault; there wasn't some technical glitch in my riding. I just didn't draw bulls you could score well on. By the time my luck changed, I was too far back to make a run.

That's the way it goes sometimes. You can go for weeks without drawing a bull or a saddle bronc you can get a good score on. Either the bull is a dud, one that doesn't kick and therefore is tough to score well on, or he's an eliminator, a bull that defies convention and is hard to ride, which is equally hard to score on. At times you can make the best ride you're capable of and the stock simply isn't good enough for you to get a great score.

I wasn't immune to bad luck, but I had an advantage. Because I competed in three events, I gave myself more chances to win. The chances of drawing a low-scoring bull, a low-scoring saddle bronc, and a low-scoring bareback were pretty slim. The odds of that happening two or three weeks in a row were extreme.

My bull riding was better in the college rodeos. We'd had a solid fall season, winning two out of the four rodeos. Odessa led the conference at the end of the first semester, and I'd had solid bull riding performances in every event. I also won the all-around titles at the Eastern New Mexico Rodeo, and the Vernon College Rodeo. It didn't help my PRCA standings, but earning those titles did wonders for my confidence going into the new year.

In the spring, our team at Odessa jelled and we were unstoppable. With Sean McMullen racking up points in the calf roping and bulldogging and our other guys putting together solid performances every week, we won six out of six rodeos that spring, and I won the all-around at all six of them. To cap off the season, we traveled to Montana State University in Bozeman for the College National Finals, where we were heavily favored, even though the host school, Montana State, was the defending national champion.

"Stay loose," Coach Watkins told us. "You've done real well all year because you haven't tightened up. If you look at this just like any other rodeo, we'll do fine."

We did more than fine. When the finals were completed, Odessa College won the College National Championship in a rout, beating Montana State by a score of 1,410 to 801. I won the bronc riding, the bull riding, and the all-around and finished second in the bareback riding. My total points for the week were 909, which meant I scored more points than the entire second-place team. Sean had 456 points in calf roping for Odessa, and our other four guys picked up the remaining 45.

At the end of the school year when the numbers were tallied, I won the all-around cowboy title with a total of 2,009 points for the year, 784 points ahead of second-place finisher Ken Lensegrav. While all records are made to be broken, I expect that one to remain intact for a few more years.

As summer finally rolled around, I felt more confident than I had in a long time. I had kept my word to Coach Watkins and done it in record fashion. We'd won the College National Championship; I'd given him two good years of riding; and when the grades were finally tallied in the late spring of 1989, I was named cum laude for my academics at Odessa. Now it was off to the next task: winning my first all-around world championship cowboy buckle in the PRCA.

One of the biggest surprises I'd found in the PRCA was the mind-set many professional cowboys took with them into the arena. A lot of guys—more than I would ever have figured—simply accepted that they weren't going to win every event at every rodeo. They were resigned that they weren't going to ride every animal they drew. Consistency was their goal. If you rode well enough throughout the year, avoiding injury and putting together okay scores and reasonable earnings, you could do well in the end. "That's just the nature of roughstock riding," they would say. "Some bulls are going to throw you no matter what you do, and sometimes other cowboys are going to make better rides than you do."

I never thought that way, and I refused to accept that attitude. Intellectually, I knew the odds were stacked against me. I knew that at the end of the year when the wins and the losses were tallied, I was going to have more losses than wins, more seconds, thirds, and fourths than victories, but that didn't mean I had to like it. I never accepted losing.

A perfect example of this was the Reno Rodeo Championship in late June. I didn't win a single event that weekend, but I rode well enough for a tie for third in the saddle bronc riding, and a berth in the finals of the bull riding. The bulls were particularly tough that weekend. Only three out of eleven bulls were ridden. A bull named Copenhagen Times threw me in the first couple of seconds. Still, I cashed a check for $5,449 in Reno that weekend and walked away with the all-around title. Was I happy? The all-around title was okay, but I wasn't thrilled at not winning any events. No-scoring in the finals of the bull riding really pissed me off. Consistency won the title for me, but it was an ugly win, one that left a kiss-your-sister taste in my mouth.

My attitude was unique, but it worked. I was leading the all-around standings going into the busiest part of the year. Life was good, and four months shy of my twentieth birthday, I was sure it was going to keep getting better. Then, out of nowhere, one day in July brought everything into perspective.

COWBOYS CALL IT "The Daddy of Them All," one of the biggest and best rodeos in the world, and the one every rising-star cowboy knows he needs to attend. The official title of the event is Cheyenne Frontier Days, and it caps the busiest month in the rodeo season, usually falling on the last weekend in July. Not only is Frontier Days one of the biggest events of the rodeo season, it's the biggest sporting event in the state of Wyoming, attracting upward of 150,000 people for the week. In 1989, I couldn't wait to get to Cheyenne. I was on a roll, riding well, and in a tight race in the all-around standings with ropers Clay O'Brien Cooper and my uncle, Butch Myers.

Jim Sharp, whose fame made him a big draw for Cheyenne organizers, was just as excited as I was about the trip. He had also been riding well and was right in the thick of a tight bull-riding race with Tuff Hedeman, Wacey Cathy, and Ervin Williams. We were riding at the top of our games. If we could just keep the momentum going through the end of the season, we thought we had a chance to bring two or three championship titles to the Bronco House. By the end of the weekend, the standings were the last thing on our minds.

As always, I traveled with Cody, and Jim traveled with Tuff and Lane. No matter how we traveled, we always stuck together. But throughout 1989 we'd showed particular support for Lane. He was having a rough time. From 1984 through 1988, he had never been out of the top ten in bull riding, and he had won the PRCA bull riding championship in 1987 at age twenty-three. Now he had fallen out of the top fifteen for the first time since his rookie season. Everybody wanted to see him get back in the hunt for the championship, so we all went out of our way to encourage him.

Lane had been a rising star from the moment he'd set foot on the PRCA circuit. He and Tuff and Cody were an inseparable threesome in those early years, but Lane had drawn most of the attention. Fans loved him, reporters and cameramen always swirled around him, and it seemed like he was always signing autographs. He'd stand in the arena for hours until every kid had an autograph. The kids still lined up, but there weren't as many reporters waiting on him these days. Lane had hit a rough patch.

We also knew that he and his wife of four years, Kellie, had been working through some troubles. The two had gone through a trial separation, but were back together by July. At the ripe old age of nineteen, I wasn't much on giving relationship advice, but I knew what it meant to be a friend to somebody who was having problems.

Lane seemed excited when he got to Cheyenne. He'd been hired to act as Scott Glenn's stunt double in a movie entitled *My Heroes Have Always Been Cowboys*. Kellie, a championship-caliber barrel racer, was in the movie as well, and the two of them appeared to be as happy as a couple could be. They were negotiating for a piece of property in Marietta, Oklahoma, close to both his and her parents, where Lane hoped to build a ranch. Everything seemed back to normal. Now all he needed was a few good rodeos to get back in contention.

Lane made it to the short round, but it was going to be a tough final day. By Sunday afternoon, the arena at Cheyenne was a mess. They'd had rain and enough riding and roping throughout the week that the place looked more like a mud-wrestling pit than a rodeo arena. The sky was still overcast, and I remember looking up and wondering if it was going to rain before the end of the day. Not that it mattered to me. As had happened all too often for my liking throughout the summer, I hadn't made it to the short round in the bull riding, but I was there, inside the arena on a pickup horse helping rope bulls, something I'd volunteered to do because I loved it. Tuff and Cody had already ridden. Jim was waiting. Lane was climbing over the railing and into his chute. It was 3:30 P.M.

The bull was named Taking Care of Business, owned by Bad Company Rodeo. I didn't know much about him, but that wasn't unusual. I didn't keep track of the bulls and broncs I rode. Cody used to laugh at me because I wouldn't know what I'd drawn until I was about to ride. There was no way I was going to know anything about a bull a friend of mine was riding. Later I learned that Taking Care of Business had been used in the 1987 NFR, where Ted Nuce had scored an 80 on him, and again in the 1988 NFR, where he'd bucked off Gary Toole.

Lane looked good getting on the bull, nothing out of the ordinary. I'd watched him ride enough times to know what was coming. As soon as he got his wrap and scooted up toward his riding hand, he was going to say, "Okay, boys! Okay, boys!" Every rider had his own way of doing things in the chute. I never said anything. I just focused on the bull and nodded my head. Whatever made the rider comfortable was the way you had to go, and Lane had always done it the same way.

I settled my horse in the back of the arena. If the bull got stubborn and refused to leave the arena after the ride, I would ride my horse forward and help the bullfighters move him through the gate.

"Okay, boys! Okay, boys!"

The chute opened, and Lane was out with what appeared to be the start of a good ride. He was wearing a blue-and-white plaid shirt and a white straw hat, and I remember thinking that with all the mud he was going to have to throw away his clothes after this ride no matter how things turned out. He also had a mouth guard because his jaw was wired shut from a wreck he'd had on a bull a month earlier in Fort Worth. At least he didn't have to worry about getting mud in his mouth, I thought.

The bull was rank, and Lane was making a good ride. I was watching Lane's form, which seemed to be exactly what you'd expect from a world champion. His right leg slid out for a fraction of a second but he recovered. Unlike me, Lane's right hand was his free hand, and he used that hand and arm to recover when the bull changed leads and tried to pull him into the well.

Despite the weather a big crowd was on hand. Die-hard rodeo fans wouldn't miss the bull riding for anything, and the folks at the arena that day were getting their money's worth. Most of the crowd got to their feet and cheered as Lane neared the eight-second mark. It was a helluva bull ride.

Lane always liked to step off a bull near its rear. He even had a video called *Bull Talk* where he said, "The bull is moving away from the rider. This gives the bullfighters a chance to distract it, and the rider a chance to get away."

He did just what he'd said in his video, letting loose of his rope and sliding off the left side of Taking Care of Business near his rear, hitting the mud, and quickly scrambling to his knees.

The bull turned quickly to his left. Before anyone could get near him, he was at Lane's back.

Lane tried to bolt out of the way. He was on his hands and knees, and he planted his right foot, trying to propel himself ahead. It didn't work. The mud in the arena was like ice.

Taking Care of Business hooked Lane near the top of his hamstrings, knocking him flat on the ground. By this time I was inching my horse forward. This didn't look that bad. Lane had been in some hellacious wrecks in his career, but he'd always got up and dusted himself off. By Lane Frost standards this didn't look that serious. Still, every cowboy has a niggling sense of anxiety when he sees a buddy down. Lane was in the most vulnerable position he could be in through no fault of his own. He'd made a great ride, and now he was on the ground with a bull over the top of him. It could have been any one of us, and we knew it.

Lane rolled to his right side and curled into the fetal position, trying to make himself as small as possible to minimize the bull's target. Then Taking Care of Business rolled his head and pushed Lane forward a few feet in the mud.

The bullfighters were doing everything they could. One

of them slapped the bull on the nose in an attempt to get his attention. They were risking their lives, just as they did every week, to save a rider. Unfortunately, Taking Care of Business was having none of it.

This had been going on for five or six seconds, an eternity when you're on the ground with a two-thousand-pound bull on your ass. Taking Care of Business bucked over Lane and the bull rope fell on top of him. By this time the bull-fighters had gained position and were waving Taking Care of Business away from Lane.

I had ridden forward and had my rope ready, not that I planned on roping Taking Care of Business; this was just a way of getting the bull's attention and getting him moving where you wanted him to go. Now that he was heading toward the gate, I turned my horse around and rode back toward the end of the arena. Lane would be fine. Jim would be in his chute and ready to ride in the next few seconds.

Lane did get up, but only for a couple of seconds. He was leaning to his left with his left arm tight against his side, but he took a step or two toward the gate. He was hurt, no doubt about it, but he was up and moving. Typical Lane. It looked as though he'd be fine.

Then he motioned with his right arm for help, and he began teetering like a freshly cut tree. Bobby Romer, one of the bullfighters, made it to Lane's side just as he collapsed. That's when I knew this was something awful. He didn't fall like a man who was exhausted or injured. He collapsed like a man who was unconscious, or worse.

Tuff was out of the gate at a dead sprint. Cody wasn't

far behind. When they rolled him over, I wondered what could possibly have caused Tuff Hedeman to go so pale.

Tuff rode with Lane to the hospital, and Cody and I weren't far behind. I still thought he would be okay. There were probably some broken bones, and maybe a cut or two. He'd probably passed out when he stood up. I was sure he'd be fine.

We were met in the emergency room by a grave-looking internist, who broke the news to both of us. Lane was gone. The bull's horn hadn't penetrated his skin, but the impact had broken his ribs. The severed ribs tore an artery. The damage to his heart was irreparable. At 3:59, twenty-nine minutes after Lane had said, "Okay, boys! Okay boys!" doctors at Memorial Hospital in Cheyenne, Wyoming, stopped resuscitation procedures and pronounced Lane Frost dead. He was twenty-five years old.

I heard what the doctor said, but at first it didn't register. How could he be dead? I'd just seen him. I'd talked to him less than an hour ago. I'd seen the wreck up close from the perfect vantage point inside the arena, and it didn't look that bad. Sure, you could never take a wreck with a two-thousand-pound bull for granted, but after years of watching cowboys get in and out of trouble, I had a pretty good handle on what was and was not a critical situation. Lane's wreck in Fort Worth had looked worse than the one that night. How could he be dead?

Cody stumbled outside and I followed him. The news was like a gut shot for the both of us. We sat on the curb and tried to catch our breath between sobs, both of us stunned and wondering what to do, what to say, whom to call, and where to go next. Tuff stayed back in the trauma center with Lane. Cody and I just sat outside and stared at a world that would never be the same.

Kellie hadn't made the trip to Cheyenne because of the pending movie deal. It was the first time she'd missed Cheyenne Frontier Days since she and Lane had been married. Now it was up to Tuff to call her and tell her what had happened. He also had to call Lane's parents, Clyde and Elsie, back in Oklahoma. Those were the toughest moments of Tuff's life, but it was his duty as Lane's friend. Tuff stayed with Lane long after he was gone, cleaning the caked mud off his friend's chaps and boots, and making sure nothing got discarded or misplaced at the hospital.

The next morning Cody and Tuff rode together to the Cheyenne airport, where they boarded a chartered plane along with the casket that held Lane's body. It was fitting that his best friends would accompany him back to Oklahoma. I wasn't far behind them.

I was as torn up as I had ever been. Sure, I'd experienced loss in my life, just as every man does, but never like this. Lane was a friend, a fellow cowboy, a champion doing what he loved—what we all loved!—who had died in the arena in front of our eyes. This was a tough road to walk for me, and it was even tougher for Jim, Tuff, and Cody. I'd known Lane from a distance for four or five years, but I'd only been close to him since I'd started riding professionally the previous season. Those guys had known him since he'd first come out. They were contemporaries, men who had struggled through this business as competitors, but also as best friends, traveling cowboys who were living the life they'd all imagined, the life they'd always dreamed of. Now one of them was gone.

On Wednesday, August 2, 1989, thirty-five hundred people made their way to the First Baptist Church of Atoka, Oklahoma, to pay their respects to Lane. At least a thousand cowboys were in attendance, hard, tough, no-nonsense men. Every one of us wept without shame.

The Oklahoman estimated that twenty-five hundred people stood in the rain outside the packed church and listened to the service over a bank of speakers. They got to hear a good one. Rodeo announcer Clem McSpadden gave a stirring eulogy. "Lane had one great quality that separated him from others of this generation today," Clem said. "He knew no greed. To the people he baled hay with in Choctaw County, and the people he worked with, he was just what he was. He had goals that far exceeded a championship buckle, and today he wears the buckle of immortality."

Under a canopy of gray clouds, Tuff, Jim, Cody, Clint Branger, Wes Ward, and Guy Sartin formed two lines on either side of the walnut casket and carried Lane to his final resting place at Mount Olivet Cemetery in Hugo, Oklahoma.

• • •

FOR A LONG TIME after losing Lane, nothing seemed natural or normal. The atmosphere on the road was thick with grief. We didn't joke the way we used to, and the travel and preparation seemed more like work than it had before. Of course we all went back to riding, because that's who we were. We all knew the risks; we always had. You don't climb on a bull without knowing you could be seriously injured or killed. That was part of the business, something we all knew in advance, but something we never talked about. If you dwelled on getting hurt, you might as well hang up your spurs. Danger was a big part of the game, but it was also something you compartmentalized, something you pushed to the back of your mind when it came time to get into the chutes. Now we'd lost a friend, and the risks of our sport had become very real to all of us.

Everybody handles grief differently. Focusing on each ride, each event, with a 100 percent intensity kept my mind sharp and helped me get through the rough times. The weekend after we buried Lane, I was back in Wyoming riding in the Gillette Rodeo, where I finished second in the saddle bronc riding and won the bareback. Sure, it was tough to go back, but it never occurred to me not to. It was even harder watching Cody, Jim, and Tuff cope, but we all pressed ahead. Lane would have kicked our asses if we'd slowed down or taken time off because of him. Nobody pretended it was easy, but we did what we had to do. We were cowboys, just like Lane.

Like a lot of tragedies, Lane's death focused a spotlight

on our sport, one that had the unintended consequence of showing people what kind of athletes we were. Despite the best efforts of champions like Larry Mahan to bring our sport into the mainstream, cowboys still weren't looked at as athletes, and rodeo wasn't considered a sport to a big bulk of people. Lane's death shone a spotlight on the physical and mental demands as well as the dangers of our game. Suddenly, the sports world looked at us a little differently.

I tried to tune out all the distractions during that time. If I could remain focused on the task at hand, making each ride the center of my mental and physical universe, I could not only get back into a routine, I could also get through the tough feelings. That attitude and focus paid off in terms of my riding. By Labor Day I was second in the all-around standings, a thousand dollars behind Butch Myers. Two weeks later those roles were reversed. I led the all-around on September 19 with $84,044, Butch was second with $82,465, and Clay O'Brien Cooper was third with $76,967. The three of us would jockey back and forth throughout the rest of the season. A few weeks I would lead, then Butch or Clay would have a good weekend and grab the lead away from me.

Suddenly, the rodeo world began to notice that we were running out of weekends, and my uncle and I were battling for the top spot in the all-around. That became the story of the fall even though the race was a lot closer than just the two of us. "He's going to be tough to beat," I told a reporter in late October. "But I think once we get to the Finals, it'll open up to a lot more guys than just me and my uncle. There's a lot of good cowboys like Lewis Field and Clay O'Brien Cooper that'll be there too."

By then it was obvious I would not only qualify for my first NFR, but I would be a contender, which is exactly what I had set out to do. This is when reporters began to ask me what I considered some of the stupidest questions I'd ever heard. "Are you looking to win in your first NFR, or are you just happy to have qualified?" one print reporter asked.

"Well, of course I'm happy I qualified, because you can't win it if you aren't there," I said. "If I wasn't going there to win, I'd stay home and watch football on television."

My answer got a laugh, but I was serious. My whole life I'd heard athletes say things like "I'm just happy to be in the Super Bowl" or "It's an honor to make it to the Final Four," which it is, but I never looked at it that way. I was happy to have made it to the NFR, but I wasn't going to get overly excited. That was just the first step. You had to be there to win, and you had to win your first one before you could win your second, third, fourth, or fifth. My career goal was to win seven world all-around titles. I couldn't reach that goal until I won my first one, and I couldn't win my first one until I qualified for the NFR. I didn't want to dismiss qualifying as "no big deal," but I looked at it as a first step, not something I should celebrate.

The follow-up question stunned me even more. "Are you going to have to step up your riding a notch now that you're in the NFR?"

I'd heard other athletes answer that question by saying

things like "Now that we're in the play-offs, we have to elevate our game to another level" or "We've got to bring it up a notch now that we're in the finals." I had no idea what those guys were talking about. If I had been a football player whose goal was to win the Super Bowl, I would have stepped it up a notch the moment the ball was kicked off in the first game of the season, and I wouldn't have let up until they were handing out championship rings. That was the way I rode. "I don't have another level," I told the reporter. "I give it all I have every time I'm out there. That's all I know. If I had to take it to another level to win, I'd be out of luck, because this is the only level I've got."

I HAVE TO ADMIT my adrenaline was pumping when I walked into the Thomas and Mack Center that December of 1989. There's electricity in the air at the NFR that you don't feel at other rodeos. Cheyenne, Denver, and Houston are big, but nothing like this. The NFR is our Super Bowl. It pits the top fifteen cowboys in each event together for ten rounds of action to determine the champions of the year. I qualified in bareback and saddle bronc riding and barely missed making it in bull riding.

I had made more money than any rodeo cowboy, which meant I got to wear the back number 1 throughout the week. But because the NFR only allowed you to count one hundred rodeos toward the all-around (and I had rodeoed in

111 at the time), some of the money I'd earned didn't count, and I trailed Clay by several hundred dollars in official earnings going into the week. And I was ahead of Butch by only the price of a good steak dinner.

Because we were competing in different events, it was almost impossible to keep up with how the points and earnings were shaking out throughout the week. Butch and Clay were competing in timed events, events where the clock was the only judge. I was riding roughstock with a different group of competitors.

I don't know how Butch and Clay felt about the three of us not competing directly against one another, but throughout my career it never bothered me. I couldn't control what any other cowboy did. If I did the best I could, I felt confident the scores and dollars would fall my way.

I didn't ride in the opening ceremonies, even though I was the leading cowboy and would have led the Texas delegation into the arena. The bareback competition started right after the opening ceremonies, so I was back in the locker room getting my rigging together and getting myself mentally ready for my first ride.

I did make it out to the arena for the Lane Frost memorial service that had been organized. Every cowboy attended this solemn event. I found it hard going through the emotions again, but after almost five months, some of the hurt had eased and many of us were happy to remember Lane again for the positive things he had done and the good things he had stood for. It was nice to sit around and talk about him with Cody, Tuff, and Jim and be able to laugh.

Once the competition began, I parked my emotions on the sidelines. I had a routine that I followed for all my rides, and I needed to get back into that routine to get myself ready to ride.

My bareback was a mare named Kattle Kate owned by Flying U Rodeo, one of about forty stock contractors that had animals at the NFR. Only the best made it to the finals. Each contractor was told which animals to bring (the best bucking stock on their herds), and they gladly obliged. Not only did the riders earn money at the finals, but payouts went to the best stock as well. Winning an award like Bucking Bull of the Year could be quite lucrative for a contractor. Season fees increased dramatically when you had a winner.

Kattle Kate wasn't going to win any awards at this NFR, but she was no dud either. I rode her well, and finished tied for sixth in the first round of bareback riding with a score of 78. It was a good start.

I didn't take a lot of time soaking up the atmosphere after that first ride. In fact, I went straight back to the locker room, where I put away my bareback rigging and got out my halter and bronc saddle. I also broke small rocks of rosin and rubbed them on the area of my chaps that would be in direct contact with my saddle. This had been my routine for years, and I wasn't about to change now.

I walked out to the chute without my halter or saddle and petted the horse I'd drawn, a big black colt named Bad River, who was owned by Harry Vold. As always, I was calm and deliberate with the animal, running my hand down his neck and talking to him in an easy voice. "Are you okay tonight?" I said to Bad River. "That's good, because I'm doing real good too." Of course the horse didn't understand me, but he understood the message. I was cool, calm, and collected and intended to stay that way. This was no big deal.

Then I put on the bronc halter from Bad River's left side. From there I didn't have to reach over the horse's head to adjust and buckle the halter. I simply dropped the halter in front of his shoulders and reached under his neck to get the strap, slowly, just as I'd done a thousand times before. Then I tucked the rein in the halter, careful not to get it too close to the horse's eyes. There was no reason to spook the animal. Once the rein was in place, I petted Bad River a few more times until he licked his lips and blinked his eyes. These were signs that the horse was relaxing. I wanted him as calm as possible until the chute opened.

I put my saddle on from above him, which is what I'd always done. I'd seen a few guys in my amateur days who'd reached through the slats to saddle a bronc. That was fine as long as the horse stayed perfectly still. If the animal jumped or shifted, you had a better than average chance of getting your arm broken doing things that way. I always worked from above the horse whenever possible.

Bad River continued to cooperate, but I kept an eye on him. I'd been around horses long enough to sense a change in temperament. If I saw something I didn't like, I would slow down and change my rhythm until the horse calmed down. When the bronc ahead of me went out, I pulled the cinch with slow, steady pressure, then I measured my rein, placing it in my hand between my thumb and index finger at exactly the spot I wanted to hold. I only measured once, as always. I figured the horse's neck wasn't going to grow in the thirty seconds or so before the chute opened.

With the rein in hand, I put my right foot (the one facing the arena) on the saddle to let Bad River know I was there. Then I sat down in the saddle, keeping some slack in the rein. If he decided to object to my presence, I didn't want him jerking the rein out of my hand.

I put my right foot in the stirrup first, then the left. Then I put my legs against the swells of the saddle and drew my feet back. Only another second or two.

Finally I took the slack out of my rein by moving it in front of me without jerking or otherwise upsetting Bad River. I made sure I was comfortably in my saddle, leaning slightly back and keeping my feet light.

Then I nodded.

Bad River committed to the air quickly, which was just fine with me. I moved my feet out and under his neck as he peaked. With momentum working for me, it was easy to get my feet set for the spur out before Bad River's front feet hit the ground.

By the third jump I was in a groove, bringing my body forward with the momentum of the jump. My knees stayed up against the swells of the saddle, but my feet were out for each spur stroke. I kept my feet back until the peak of each jump; then I moved them forward and leaned my body back, flowing with the horse's momentum as if we were one unit.

My free arm was like a lever, pulling my body forward at the pinnacle of each jump, then helping move me back as Bad River peaked and kicked.

When the whistle blew, I knew I'd made a great ride. The pickup man was at my side in an instant. Because Bad River was still bucking, it was easier to get onto the pickup horse. I simply used the momentum of a jump to propel me onto the pickup horse. I grabbed the pickup man around his midsection and held on as we cleared the bronc's path.

A few seconds later, after Bad River had left the arena, the scores went up. I'd scored a 77, a good ride, and with the 78 I'd already gotten, it was a great start to the week.

I improved as the week progressed. By the end of the fourth round of saddle bronc riding, I had a first and two seconds. Through six rounds of bareback riding I had one win and two thirds. With four rounds to go I had jumped into the all-around lead and was riding as well as anyone. If I stuck with it, I knew I could win.

My scores dropped in rounds seven and eight, but in the ninth round I made a good saddle bronc ride on Copenhagen Joe, finishing fourth in the round with a score of 75. I'd also put together solid bareback rides, posting scores in each round even though my best finish was a tie for seventh in the eighth round when I scored a 74 on a rank bronc named Skoal Exorcist. Things were still pretty close going into the final round, or so I gathered from what the press was telling me. I wasn't following the other scores. I was leading with one round to go. My destiny was in my hands. If I put together two good rides, I knew I would win my first all-around world championship.

That Sunday morning as I put on my boots and prepared to head to the arena, I kissed my girlfriend at the time good-bye and said, "When you see me again, I'll be the world champion." She smiled and didn't say anything. What could you say to something like that? The scores were still close, and I couldn't control what Butch or Clay did in the final round. Butch had no-times (which meant he'd missed his calf and hadn't posted a time) in four of the first nine rounds of the calf roping, but he had a first and a second and had posted a time in every round of the bulldogging.

Clay was only competing in team roping, but he had done pretty well all week. He and his partner, Jake Barnes, had two seconds, a first, and a fourth.

When I saw my mom that morning, she was as tense as I'd ever seen her. When I was growing up, I always asked Mom if she was nervous when I rode. "No," she said. "I never get nervous." It wasn't until I saw television tapes of her expressions that I knew she was lying. Before Sunday's final round, she didn't make any pretense.

Bareback riding was my first event of the day. I drew a horse called Rabbit, a Mesquite Championship Rodeo–owned bronc I knew absolutely nothing about. He turned out to be good, and I scored a 78 and finished the round tied for sixth. That was enough to split second and third in the bareback average for the week, which paid a huge bonus and elevated my lead to the point where I was almost out of reach.

It all came down to my bronc ride. I didn't have to win the round, but I needed a good score to clinch the world title. That didn't stop me from riding to win. I wasn't about to go conservative on the final ride of the year.

The horse was a mare named Oil City Red. She was famous for her first four jumps. After that you could get a good rhythm on her. A lot of guys never made it that far. I did. When the scores went up, I saw that I'd scored a 73, a good ride given how rank the mare was, but not good enough to win the round.

It was good enough to give me a sixth place finish in the overall saddle bronc average. I didn't know if that was enough for the all-around championship, but I had a good feeling about it. I'd done everything I could.

Dad was always the scorekeeper in the family. Mom and I never had the patience for it, but Dad always kept his tally sheet nearby with all the standings, the earnings, and the possible scenarios mapped out like a scorecard. After I got off Oil City Red and my score went up on the board, he did some quick calculations while Mom sat nervously next to him. After a second or two he said, "He just won the world championship!"

Mom was having none of it. "I'm not listening to you. I'll not believe it until I hear it from somebody official."

Twenty minutes later she had her answer. An official of the PRCA found Mom and Dad in the stands and extended his hand. "Congratulations. Ty's won the world all-around championship."

At twenty years and two months, I was the youngest man ever to win the PRCA world all-around championship, edging out Jim Shoulders, who'd won his first title in 1949 at age twenty-one. I was also the first cowboy in history to win a national college all-around title and a PRCA world all-around championship in the same year. But those records weren't as important to me as earning that first gold world-championship buckle. "It sure is pretty," I said to the assembled crowd when they presented me with that first buckle.

Now I could celebrate. The season was over.

THAT NIGHT, the Coors Brewing Company honored Lane Frost with the annual Coors Favorite Cowboy Award, an honor normally voted on by the fans. This year Coors had changed the rules. There was only one cowboy worthy in 1989. Kellie Frost accepted the award and the $3,000 check, sharing the moment with Clyde and Elsie Frost, who were also in attendance.

Ask any cowboy about 1989 and the first words out of his mouth will always be "That's the year we lost Lane." That's how it should be. Lane meant a lot to many people, and he meant a lot to the future of our sport. In some strange way, his death brought cowboys more recognition and appreciation.

In 1994, Lane's life was put on the big screen in a movie called *8 Seconds*. Luke Perry played Lane in the film, and Cody, Tuff, and I consulted on the project from the script development all the way through postproduction. As is always the case when a true story is being made into a movie, there were arguments. Cody called the director a "stupid little peckerhead" so many times the poor guy quit twice. But we were passionate about making the movie a success. Lane was our friend. We were determined to ensure his memory was properly honored.

After the season was over, I had to say I was happy. I had ended the eighties by winning my first PRCA world championship. I'd beaten the best of the best and proven to the world and to myself that I was a contender at the top levels of our sport. But I had one less friend to share my victory with. No matter how many toasts we drank in the months that followed, there was always a tinge of sadness in our group. There was one empty chair at the table, one less number to draw when the dinner check arrived.

I had won a world title, but we all had lost a friend. A closetful of championship buckles would never make that hurt go away.

6

Tying the Record

MY MOM AND DAD always told me that if I wasn't paying attention to where I was going, chances were pretty good I wouldn't end up where I wanted to be. They also taught me the value of learning from the mistakes of others. If you see a mistake, you don't have to repeat it to learn from it. Even as a kid that made sense. As a world champion these were lessons I drew on often.

The first challenge I faced was the increased demands on my time. When you're the world champion, every reporter at every rodeo wants to interview you; every rodeo promoter wants you to attend his event; every hat, shirt, jean, boot, spur, and saddle company wants you to wear or use its products; and every fan wants you to stop what you're doing, sign a few pictures, and chat about everything from bull-rope rosin to the length of your stirrups. It's easy to lose focus, especially when people shower you with praise and tell you how much you've meant to them. Over the years, a lot of guys have lost perspective. That's part of why only a handful of cowboys have repeated as all-around champions in the seventy-five-year history of the PRCA. In sixty years, only three guys had successfully defended their titles more than once. Jim Shoulders won it four consecutive times from 1956 through 1959. Larry Mahan won five in a row from 1966 through 1970, then won his sixth title in 1973. Tom Ferguson won six all-around world championships in a row from 1974 through 1979. A few other guys won two in a row over the years, but there are a lot more onetime champions than repeat winners. Dave Appleton, a friend and traveling partner of mine who also preceded me as world champion, didn't even qualify for the NFR in 1989 after winning it in 1988. That was a mistake I didn't want to make.

I never felt a lot of additional pressure to repeat as world champion. A lot of Super Bowl teams have trouble repeating because everybody is gunning for them. Cowboys gunned for you too, but I didn't have to line up across the ball from them. A bull or bucking horse doesn't know who you are or what you've won. Each ride is unique. The pressure I put on myself was to make each ride the best of my life. I'd won my first world title paying little or no attention to the standings, and for the next five years, I did exactly the same thing. Most of the time I had no idea where I stood. I figured I was leading because I was riding well, but unless a reporter or a member of my family filled me in on the standings, I would have no idea if I had a $2 lead or a

$200,000 blowout. Either way, I could do nothing about it other than bear down. As long as I was taking it one ride at a time, putting everything I had into every ride I made, I was doing all I could do. If I won, great. If I didn't win, there was nothing more I could do about it.

As for the distractions, I never let them bother me because I made a conscious decision not to change my style or my personality for anybody no matter how many world titles I won. There was a time when I didn't know what "just be yourself" meant. Of course you had to be yourself. Who else could you be? But when I watched other guys get caught up in the trappings of success, molding their personalities to whatever situation they were in, I realized what that phrase meant.

"How has being a world champion changed you?"

I had been asked that question a zillion times. Every time I said the same thing: "It hasn't. I'm the same guy now as I was yesterday, last month, or last year. The only thing that's changed is people's perception of me. I've never been somebody who walks into a room and takes over. I'm not quiet, but I'm not what you'd call gregarious, either. I was this way when I was sixteen; I was this way at twenty; and I'll probably be this way when I'm sixty. People who know me know that's just the way I am. And people who don't know me sometimes form opinions based on what they think I ought to be."

That might not have been the most politically correct answer, but it was the truth.

• • •

I NEVER SET out to revolutionize the sport of rodeo, but in my first few championship years I made some choices that brought change to our game. The first controversial decision I made came less than a month after I'd won my first all-around world title. Jim and I had moved out of the Bronco House and rented a place in Benbrook, Texas, just south of Fort Worth. The boxes weren't unpacked when the phone rang and a product rep for a worldwide clothing company was on the line. "Ty," he said, "as the world all-around champion, we'd like to offer you a contract."

"Okay," I said. "What's the contract?"

"We're prepared to offer you twenty-five hundred dollars and all the clothes you can wear for the year you are world champion."

"No thanks," I said without hesitation. This was a great company, but this was not the way I wanted to do business.

"Excuse me?"

"Thanks, but I'm going to pass."

"But . . . but this is the deal we've had with world champions for years. It's a very good, fair offer."

"I'm sure it is, and I appreciate you calling, but I'm going to pass." We chatted for a few more minutes; then I politely slipped in the message that if he had any more business offers, he should call my agent in California.

An agent! Who did I think I was, Michael Jordan? Cowboys didn't have agents, and they didn't blow off good deals.

Me and my dad on my first birthday. *(Murray family)*

Riding the family couch with Uncle Alvie
and my dad sitting beside me. *(Murray family)*

In my mind this wasn't riding a calf in my backyard with Dad
holding on to my belt—it was the tenth round at the National
Finals Rodeo for a world championship. Of course,
I was only two years old. *(Murray family)*

Winning the PRCA Rookie of the Year
in 1988. *(Murray family)*

Tuff Hedeman, Cody Lambert, and me
waiting to ride behind the chutes
at a PBR event. *(Kendra Santos)*

Cheyenne Frontier Days is one of the biggest and best rodeos in the world. Here I am taking my wrap on a bull in the chute at Cheyenne in 1998. *(Shari Van Alsburg)*

Here's where the eight seconds starts: I'm leaving the chute
on a bull at the PBR Finals in 2001. *(Shari Van Alsburg)*

I completed this ride on Bad Moon at the George Paul Memorial
Bull Riding event in Del Rio, Texas, in 1996, but in the process
I tore the ligament in the shoulder of my free arm. *(David Jennings)*

Lying back and enjoying the sunshine in Tucson, Arizona. *(Shari Van Alsburg)*

Aggressiveness is the key in bareback riding. *(Shari Van Alsburg)*

As with any sport, fans are a huge part of rodeo. *(Shari Van Alsburg)*

"Razor" Jim Sharp and I have remained the best of friends since our days as college roommates in Odessa. Here we are at the PBR Finals in 1999. (Jim's the one with the big ears.) *(Bert Entwistle)*

Since the beginning of time cowboys had taken whatever had been offered to them and thanked their lucky stars to get it. Boot companies used to say, "Hey, cowboy, if you let us use your name and likeness in our advertisements, we'll give you ten free pairs of boots!" The cowboys would say, "Gosh, that's a great deal. Where do I sign?"

Cowboys had always been the Spartans of sports. That was part of the mystique of our profession. The day I turned pro, I decided I wasn't going to do things that way. I had watched the world of athletics change. I'd seen guys like Jordan, Magic Johnson, Nolan Ryan, and Andre Agassi sign million-dollar deals to endorse everything from underwear to cameras. While I had no illusions about rodeo cowboys competing at that level, I knew we weren't being properly marketed or adequately compensated. I wanted to do whatever I could to change that. I had once been a kid who idolized Larry Mahan. If Larry had worn pink fur coats and eaten Weetabix cereal, I would have worn and eaten exactly the same things. Long before Nike started their "Be like Mike" campaign, I wanted to be like Larry. Now other kids probably wanted to be like me or Tuff or Cody. Maybe cowboys weren't as well-known as the Jordans, Ryans, and Agassis of the world, but we had a fan base and our names and likenesses had value that wasn't being maximized. I never blamed companies for negotiating in their own best interests, but if I was going to align myself with a corporation or a product, I had to find out what I was worth in the market.

At first you'd have thought I had burned the flag. Word spread through the rank and file that not only had I hired an agent, I had stiff-armed one of the biggest corporate supporters in rodeo. "Oh," I heard a lot of the suppliers say at rodeos throughout the year. "Can't talk to Ty. He's got an agent." This was always said in a singsong "Can you believe this?" tone. Nobody else had an agent. Why was I so special?

Today a majority of professional cowboys have agents. Still, folks couldn't believe some of the things I did back then. After my second world championship, the same clothing rep came back. This time he made an unprecedented offer for a cowboy. The company would pay me $20,000 and all the clothes I could wear for the year. Again, I said no. When I won my third world title in a row, they came back again with a $30,000 offer. Once again, I turned them down. This had nothing to do with the company. This was about establishing value for my name, and sticking to my guns.

Cowboys were shaking their heads. In their eyes I was either arrogant, crazy, or both. Even my dad couldn't believe it. "What are you thinking?" he said after I told him about the offer. "Do you have any idea how much money that is? All they want you to do is wear their clothes and let them take a couple of pictures. It's not like you're digging a ditch."

"I know, Dad," I said. "But my name and likeness are products that have value. I have to establish that value and stick with it. I can't be letting one guy use my picture for one price, and another guy sign me for another price. I have to be consistent. There's only one all-around world champion right now, and that's me. There's a fair-market value for associating with a world champion. I'm not being greedy, but right's right."

"I hope you know what you're doing."

"I do," I said, but in truth I had no idea. No cowboy had ever done what I was doing. I knew that expanding the sport was the right thing, and elevating the professionalism of our endorsement deals was something that should have happened years before, but who was I to change things? Larry had won six world titles and moved the sport closer to the mainstream than it had ever been before. Yet almost twenty years after Larry had won his last title, clothing companies' standard offer to a world champion was $2,500 and all the clothes he could wear.

I took a big gamble by bucking tradition, but it paid off. I was selective and patient in forming partnerships with companies. I also chose corporate partners that would broaden my exposure outside the world of rodeo. Sure I could have had a spur contract or a bull rope named after me, but there wasn't a big market for those items outside the rodeo world. I chose to go with companies like Post, who put my picture on a box of raisin bran. Then I signed with No Fear sportswear, where I was marketing myself alongside snowboarders, freestyle skateboarders, and surfers. I positioned myself as a cowboy, but also as an extreme athlete, somebody who could be thought of alongside Tony Hawk and Mark Fawcett as well as Cody Lambert and Tuff Hedeman.

Over the years the relationships I've had with Post raisin bran, TXU Energy, CLS Limousines, Las Vegas Convention and Visitors Authority, No Fear sportswear, Sierra Sports, MGM Grand, Wrangler, Resistol, US Smokeless Tobacco, and Dan Post Boots have been extraordinary. The long-term friends and business partners I've made have enriched my life greatly. But in those first few years, nobody would have guessed how things would turn out. I took a risk. Fortunately, I wasn't betting my livelihood on it.

HIRING AN AGENT and signing endorsement deals was never my primary concern. If I didn't continue to win championships, nobody would want me endorsing their product anyway. Expectations grow when an athlete signs a big deal. Some guys do okay, but others crumble under the scrutiny. Fortunately, I didn't feel any pressure. All I cared about was riding.

I also had plenty of help staying grounded. At the awards banquet in Colorado Springs, after I won my first world all-around title, I got a Western Union telegram from Dean "Doc" Pavillard, who had been my dad's best friend throughout my life, and who had been like a godfather to me. "Congratulations on your big win," Doc's note read. "But try to remember that hat sizes shrink with age, even if you have endorsed the hat. I am proud of you, and I love you."

This was Doc's way of telling me not to get too big-headed. I kept the note for the rest of my career and still have it to this day. Yellow and faded, it's a constant reminder of the perspective I need to have on life. Doc couldn't be at 1989 NFR, nor could he come to Colorado Springs. He was battling stomach cancer, too weak to travel. Two weeks after he wired his note, Doc was dead.

If the death of a lifelong friend wasn't enough to keep me on solid footing, I still had Cody traveling with me every week, riding my ass as if I were a rookie. By my third year I'd learned to sift through all the stuff Cody threw at me. Underneath the crusty surface, I found a great, funny friend. Our friendship didn't stop him from giving me endless grief, but then I'd read a quote like the one he gave to *Parade* magazine: "Ty is the best athlete that's ever been in our sport. He's got balance, strength, coordination, determination, and he loves his job. He really likes being a cowboy. I think he's on his way to being the best that's ever been."

I could never ask him about comments like that because I knew he'd say something like "Don't let it go to your head, you little bastard." Now I could laugh when he said things like that. I knew he would knock me off my perch if I got too high on myself.

One part of Cody's quote was indisputable: I loved my job. The very fact that it was a job was unbelievable to me. My whole life I'd paid to go to rodeos. Now I was being paid to ride. I couldn't imagine a better life. I didn't have to worry about school, didn't have to carry Finance 401 textbooks on the road with me, and didn't have to call any teachers to tell them I would be missing class. Now I was a career cowboy. When I filled out forms at the bank, under the line that said "employer" I could put "self" and under "occupation" I got a kick out of writing "cowpoke." I was making a living as a self-employed cowpoke, and loving every minute of it.

MY FIRST GOAL for 1990 was to improve my bull riding. I'd missed qualifying for the NFR in that event my first year and I didn't want to be left out again. I took it as a challenge to qualify for the finals in all my events, even though nobody had been to the NFR in three roughstock events since Larry Mahan had done it in 1973. That didn't deter me. I'd already made it once in bareback and saddle bronc riding. If I could get my bull riding up to par, I should be able to make it to the NFR as a three-event cowboy.

I picked up a lot of early momentum winning the all-around title at the season-opening National Western Stock Show in Denver. By the end of January, I was in the top five in the world in bull riding and held a healthy lead in the all-around standings.

Then in Rapid City, South Dakota, I put together one of the best bull rides of my life on one of the rankest bulls in history. Mr. T was considered the top bull in the world, and the most dreaded draw by many of the cowboys. He was big, strong, unpredictable, and mean.

I never dreaded him, but prior to Rapid City, I'd never drawn him either. I knew that he'd been ridden only once, the previous July when Marty Staneart had stayed on him at Cheyenne Frontier Days. Prior to that, he'd thrown 187 cowboys, including 10 at the NFR. Jim Sharp had drawn him in the tenth round of the 1989 NFR when he and Tuff were in a battle for the bull riding title. Mr. T had thrown Jim in two seconds, breaking my roommate's string of twenty-three consecutive successful bull rides at the NFR. Now I was in the chute getting my bull rope tightened around Mr. T's massive black-and-white body.

When the chute opened, Mr. T jumped out and spun to his right quickly, almost too quickly I thought. I wasn't sure we were clear of the chute when he started spinning. Not only was he a strong, athletic bull, he was smart. He knew where I was at all times. One round he would try to pull me into the well (the imaginary circle on the inside of a bull's spin); the next round he would speed up and try to sling me to the outside. But my free arm moved with him, and I was able to anticipate and stay in the middle of him throughout the ride. I felt comfortable on him the entire time.

Then I heard something only one other person had ever heard while on this bull's back: the whistle.

I stepped off Mr. T and threw my hat in the air, something I almost never did, but I couldn't help myself. This ride was a jump start to my year, a catapult that gave me the confidence I needed to keep my bull riding at the highest possible level.

• • •

I GOT ON A ROLL, winning the all-around titles at big rodeos like Colorado Springs, Phoenix, and in the Astrodome at the Houston Livestock Show, one of the biggest rodeos in the country, to name a few. The Houston win cost me though. The same night I was scheduled to ride in Houston I was supposed to compete in the short round of the saddle bronc and bull riding at the San Antonio Livestock Show and Rodeo, another big-time event. I was booked on a commercial flight from Houston to San Antonio as soon as I finished my ride. But there was a problem. Country singer Clint Black was performing in the Astrodome in front of his hometown crowd prior to the saddle bronc riding. The crowd loved him and kept calling him back for encores. The third time Clint came back onto the stage, I knew I'd missed my flight. It cost me at least $10,000 in potential winnings (I had a 16-point lead), not to mention a pickup truck I would have won if I'd taken the all-around in San Antonio. Then there was the cost of an unused airline ticket. Oh, and Clint's final song was "Killin' Time." I listened to it with my head in my hands, knowing that was exactly what he'd done to me.

Each week I felt my riding improve. By early May my bull riding was at the same level as my bareback and saddle bronc riding. Everything clicked. I just needed to keep it up and avoid injury, which was a pretty tall order.

It doesn't matter how many animals you've ridden in

your life, accidents can happen in a heartbeat. It's usually something freakish and small, like a hanging spur or a slip in the mud. Even the best cowboys can't control those incidents. On May 19, 1990, I experienced one such incident firsthand. At the time I was leading the all-around standings at the Redding Rodeo in Redding, California, and was thinking about extending my overall lead in the standings.

I'd drawn a saddle bronc named Road Agent, a good horse I felt comfortable about. He was one of those horses I connected with, the kind of animal I knew I could anticipate and ride well. He was also a little showy, which made it easier to get a good score on him.

This time was no exception. When the chute opened, Road Agent jumped one time then immediately started spinning as well as bucking. I made a great ride on him, scoring 72 points. I felt great about the night.

Then as I was making a move to get off the horse, my left foot hung in the stirrup for an instant. Just like that, I was whipped underneath.

In a split second I was facedown in the mud, stunned by the quick turn of events. Then I felt a whack against the back of my head and the warm sting of blood flowing from underneath my hairline. A second later I felt a thud against my side. I knew the horse had stepped on me.

But it was the final kick that did the real damage. As I was trying to scramble out of the way, Road Agent kicked one more time and his hoof caught me on the right elbow. Pain went through my arm like I'd been shot. At first I thought I'd just gotten thumped on the funny bone, but as my arm swelled, I knew it was serious.

My head required four stitches, and the doctors at Justin Sports Medicine insisted that I wear a wrap around my ribs. But my elbow was broken. Cody found me in the medical center as the doctor was putting my arm in a sling. "Don't think this gets you out of driving," he said.

As Cody pointed out, I could drive a car with a broken elbow, and I could still ride roughstock with bruised ribs and stitches in my head, but a broken bone in my riding arm was a sidelining injury. I was out for almost six weeks. Still, I tried to remain upbeat. As I told a reporter at the time, "I ain't gonna rush anything. I've got a comfortable lead, so there's no hurry. A lot of guys try to hurry things up and they make them worse. When the elbow gets ready, I'll be back out there. Fortunately, this is about the only injury I've had."

It wasn't the only injury I would have that year, though. As predicted, I came back in early July with my elbow in a brace, but I continued to rack up points and cash checks. Riding with braces and wraps was nothing unusual in our sport. In fact, you were something of a freak if you didn't have something wrapped, taped, or braced when you went into the arena.

My first week back, I wore a brace and a wrap. It felt a little different, but it didn't impede my movement. If anything, I felt stronger with the brace on. I won the saddle bronc riding and all-around title at the Reno Rodeo. I qualified for the NFR by finishing fifth in the standings in bull riding, sixth in saddle bronc, and seventh in bareback. I could check off one goal for the year: I'd become the third cowboy in history and the first in seventeen years to qualify for the NFR in all three roughstock events.

Now another challenge emerged. I went to Las Vegas having won $141,000 in one hundred rodeos. No cowboy in history had ever won $200,000 in one year. If I could reach that mark, I felt that I could accomplish two tasks: I'd break the all-time earnings record, and I would win my second consecutive all-around world championship.

All I needed was a good week to lock up the title. But good wasn't good enough. I entered the NFR like every other rodeo: to win.

On opening night of the NFR I felt as comfortable as I had in a long time. Las Vegas, the Thomas and Mack Center, the setup, and all the hoopla surrounding the NFR had become familiar to me now. It was like visiting an old friend. Only this time I was here as defending champion.

The first round I tied for second in the bull riding and bareback. The next day Cody and I split first place in the saddle bronc round. I placed fourth in the second round of bull riding that night as well.

I continued to ride well in every event, which was my main goal. The three roughstock events are so different, each requiring its own set of skills and disciplines, that being equal in all three was, for me, a great accomplishment. Bareback riding is more about strength, flexibility, and aggressiveness. Saddle bronc riding is about timing, balance, and form (sort of like the compulsory exercises in gymnastics or figure skating). Bull riding is about anticipating, reacting, and staying in control in a powerful and scary environment. I had honed my skills in all three events to the point where I didn't favor one over the other. Sure, at times I woke up so sore I couldn't get out of bed after competing in three events, but that never dampened my enthusiasm. As long as I was at the top of my game in all three events, I felt confident I would continue to win.

On Friday, December 7, Pearl Harbor Day, and the eighth day of the NFR, I had one of the best bareback rides of the year, scoring 84 points on a horse called Sippin' Velvet. That was good enough to win the round, and with it, to set a new rodeo milestone. I was the first cowboy in history to win over $200,000, having earned $203,552 with two rounds left to go.

More importantly for me, it insured that I'd won my second all-around world championship. Nobody could catch me. That didn't mean I would let up in the final two rounds. As I said to the reporters that night, "I'm real tickled this happened, but it's not about the money. I don't say, 'I'm going out to the rodeo tonight, and I'm going to break the two-hundred-thousand mark.' I'd do this for nothing. That's how I got started and it's why I do it today. Winning two hundred thousand feels good, but I just came here to make the best rides that I can."

The next night I had my second serious wreck of the

year, one that hushed the crowd and sent nervous shudders through my family and friends. My saddle bronc that night was a twelve-hundred-pound gelding named Bo Skoal, and I could sense early on that the horse wasn't right. When I'd gone out to pet him, he seemed skittish, and he didn't like it at all when I put the halter on him. As I climbed into the chute and put my foot on his back, he jumped around a little. I wanted to get out of the chute quickly on this one. He was unhappy with his life at that moment and I wasn't making things any better.

I felt that I'd calmed him down by the time I sat on him, but when I got my feet in the stirrups, I could sense that he was about to throw a fit. I wanted to get out of the chute before he had a tantrum in such tight quarters.

I nodded for the gate men to go ahead and open the chute. But as the gate opened, the horse reared up against the slats and pawed at the sky. Then in a split second he flipped over backward into the arena. If I had been pinned under the horse, I might have broken my back, but I managed to slide my body out of the animal's path, but my right knee got caught. Bo Skoal slammed on top of my knee, then rolled over it several times as he flailed around.

"I don't care how long you've been around rodeo," my dad said, "it scares you when you see something like that." Mom and Dad were petrified by what they'd seen. I was lying in the dirt consumed by a white-hot pain that made me want to scream.

A collective gasp went out from the eighteen-thousand

spectators, followed by an eerie silence. Nobody, including me, knew my status. My guess was that my knee was broken.

No bones were, in fact, broken, but my knee swelled to the size of a football. A severe bone bruise was what Dr. Tandy Freeman, one of the best orthopedic specialists in the country and the number one physician on the pro rodeo circuit, called it.

"Can I ride tomorrow?" I asked Tandy.

"It's up to you, but I'd have to say it's not likely," he said. "If the swelling goes down and you can move it, maybe. But it's a pretty severe bruise. I'd bet against it."

Tandy's staff worked on me all night and most of the next day with ice, electronic stimulation, massage, even acupuncture. In the end, Tandy was right.

I waited as long as I could before making the call. Two hours before the start of the bareback riding, I was in the training room with my leg in a muscle stimulator and ice packs wrapped around my knee. I had already won the all-around, and I'd broken an earnings record, but I still wanted to go. I might win the saddle bronc title, and I was sure I'd pick up some substantial money in the averages and go-arounds. There was a chance I could push the benchmark up to $300,000. But as the minutes crept by, I realized it was a lost cause. I couldn't bend my knee to spur.

"You going?" Colin Murnion, a bareback rider who was getting his wrist iced on the table next to me, asked.

"Doesn't look like it."

"Is it broke?"

"Nope, but I can't move it." Then I stared out at nothing and reflected on where I was, where I'd been, and where I was going. I'd won the all-around, set all kinds of records, and other than a bum knee and a broken elbow I'd gotten out of the year relatively unscathed. Sure it was disappointing not to finish the tenth round of the NFR, but I'd be back. There was always 1991, another year to think about, and another title to contest. All in all, things were pretty good. I turned back to Colin and said, "You know what? I'll bet they have this again next year."

They did, and when the final dollars were tallied, I was right in the hunt again in 1991.

FOR THE NEXT four years I won the all-around world cowboy title by some pretty solid margins. In 1991, I broke my own record, earning $244,000. In 1992, I won again with $225,000. And 1993 and 1994 were more of the same.

The money was incidental by that point. I had become the first cowboy to win over a million dollars, but I never obsessed about the money. The only reason I knew the year-end totals was because that is how the PRCA kept score. Every dollar is a point. At the end of the year the cowboy with the most money wins. Were it not for the scorekeeping aspect (and that I still had to sign my tax forms every year), I wouldn't have known how much I'd earned.

A few rides stood out, though. In 1991, doing some of

the best riding of my life, I won the bareback riding at the Cow Palace in San Francisco with a total of 255 points on three horses.

In the short go, I drew a horse named Border Town owned by the Pinz Rodeo Company. He was one of the rankest barebacks I'd ever been on, spinning so fast he looked like a bull. I rode him for all I was worth, making what was, by far, the best ride of my career.

When the scores went up, everybody went wild. I'd scored a 92, the second-highest score ever on a bareback in a PRCA-sanctioned rodeo.

Then there was Nashville, where I rode a rank paint bull called Gunslinger. I was the only person who'd ever ridden him, and he had thrown over a hundred cowboys. That day I rode him again and scored a 93.

There were plenty of great rides, plenty of tough bulls and rank bucking horses, tons of close competitions, and lots of wrecks over the years, but when I look back, the moments I remember are the ones where I put out my best stuff and reaped the rewards.

I also remember the great times with my friends. I enjoyed myself when I was out on the road. That doesn't mean I went hog wild every night, but Cody, Jim, and I spent more than a few hours in some of the finer drinking establishments this country has to offer. I never stayed out so late that it affected my riding, and I always tried to stay in control, but I've had my share of fun.

When I was competing, I never played the odds or

developed game plans for winning. My only strategy was to try my guts out every time I climbed over the chute. I proved that in 1993 in the fifth round, the toughest roughstock round of the NFR, when I drew a bull named Dodge Magnum.

The fifth and tenth rounds are the toughest. The premium bucking stock is held back until those rounds. Still, I was extremely happy with my draw. I'd ridden Dodge Magnum earlier in the year in Nampa, Idaho, and scored a 92 on him.

When the chute opened this time, I felt a sudden shift and the bull fell on his side. He recovered, and I stayed on him, but the ride was all but ruined. I scored a 65. The score didn't discourage me, though, because I knew I would get a reride.

The only question was, would I take it?

"Why take a chance on a reride?" one of the cowboys behind the chutes said to me. "You've already got fourth place locked up."

This was a risk. If I took the reride and got bucked off, I won nothing, but I didn't think that way. "I didn't come here to win fourth," I said.

Many of the people in the stands were asking the same question. If I took a chance with a reride, I risked not placing at all. As it was, I had a respectable fourth-place finish in the bag.

Dad knew what I was going to do. "He'll take the reride," he said to Mom.

I did, indeed, take the reride. The draw was Edward Scissorhands, a Canadian bull that had never been ridden. It was a huge gamble. If I stuck with my score of 65, I would make $3,500 and lock up fourth in the bull riding. But fourth wasn't first. I had a chance to win the world champion bull rider title that year, and I wasn't going to give it up by playing the percentages.

When I nodded my head, the chute opened and Edward Scissorhands burst into the arena like somebody had set off a stick of dynamite under him. I stayed loose and steady on him, never coming close to being thrown, even when he spun hard into my hand. When the whistle blew, I had scored 80 points on him, which was good enough to move me into second place.

Later that night, Mom and Dad were waiting in their seats for the crowd to clear the auditorium when a silver-haired cowboy walked down to where they were sitting. "Butch," he said, extending his hand. "Jim Shoulders. Tonight showed me why Ty is the best cowboy that's ever been."

"You hear nice things from people a lot, especially when it's your kid," Dad would later say. "But coming from Jim Shoulders, I thought it was a helluva compliment."

Five days later, when the points and the winnings were tallied, I won the bareback average and the all-around titles by healthy margins. I also won my first bull riding world title by a grand total of $95. Without the fifth-round reride I would have been an also-ran.

• • •

EVEN AFTER SIX consecutive world all-around titles, I never allowed outside pressures to affect me, but the more I won, the more distractions I had to contend with. Jealousy was one of the biggest things I found. My friends weren't jealous—at least not that they let on—and guys like Cody and Jim would never have considered such a feeling. But plenty of guys would make a point of finding me after I'd been thrown or after I'd had a bad weekend. They'd say things like "Heard you had a rough one" or "Hey, I heard you got bucked off. Hard luck." When I won, they would act like they hadn't heard the news, but they never withheld comment when I had a tough go.

Then there was the media. For five years, I'd been the darling of the press. I'd been featured in *Sports Illustrated*, *Parade*, *Reader's Digest*, *Vanity Fair*, *TV Guide*, *Texas Monthly*, *Health & Fitness*, the *Boston Globe*, and the *New York Times*, and I'd had segments on every television network, as well as ESPN. No cowboy had ever been more accommodating to the media. But a few reporters, for reasons I will never understand, decided to try to knock me off the pedestal they had placed me on.

A reporter from the *Denver Post* named Steve Lipsher showed particularly poor judgment and low standards. My relationship with Lipsher started when he called me at home (on an unlisted number) at 9 P.M. As politely as I could, I told him I'd see him in Denver at the rodeo where I'd be happy to answer his questions.

We met the following weekend, where the guy was a complete ass. He baited me, prodded me, and did everything he could to rile me up. Once again I did everything I could to be accommodating, even though I wanted to rearrange the little greaseball's hairline.

A week later, as I was unpacking in my hotel room at Steamboat Springs, where I hoped to get in a little skiing, the phone rang. I thought it was the concierge checking on my room. Unfortunately, it was Lipsher. At that point I told the guy to lose my number and burn the tapes. I wanted nothing more to do with him.

The headline of his piece was "Ty Murray Shows Signs of Fraying at 25."

Later, I had to deal with Lipsher again, this time over an incident I still find amusing. It all started in January of 1994 when I was in Denver relaxing for a couple of days before the rodeo. My uncle Chet Hier invited me up to a ranch belonging to a friend of his for a day on the snowmobiles. I'd never ridden a snowmobile so I was looking forward to it. The rancher, a fellow named Jodi Hill, was nice enough. He and his wife gave us some tips on where to ride, and they offered us drinks. It was all very hospitable.

Chet and I had a great time. I'd never realized how difficult it was to turn those snowmobiles in the deep stuff. We rode out into a clearing where, in the distance, we saw a herd of elk.

"Hey, you want to bulldog an elk?" Chet said.

"Sure," I said. What was the harm? We probably

couldn't catch one anyway, and even if we did, bulldogging wouldn't hurt it. They were huge.

We gunned our snowmobiles toward the herd. Chet swung around and broke a cow away from the herd and sent her running toward a meadow. Then he ran his machine on the hazer side and I pulled up on the bulldogging side as if we were at a rodeo.

When I got close enough, I jumped off my snowmobile and tried to grab the elk around the neck. But when I touched her, she stopped cold. I tumbled head over tail through the snow and came up looking like a snowman.

I didn't spend a lot of time dusting myself off. The elk took off again, and we hopped back on our snowmobiles to give it another shot.

This time we were successful. I made my jump a little sooner and a little closer than I would have if we'd been bulldogging a steer. I grabbed the cow around the neck and she dragged me all through the snow until I got her down.

We laughed and I petted her for a few minutes. Jodi came out and took pictures. After the elk calmed down a little, I climbed on her back and rode her for about eight seconds. She bucked and jumped, then I hopped off and she ran back into the trees where the herd had headed. It was a fun afternoon. No harm done.

A year later, I was back in Denver at an autograph signing a few days before the same rodeo. During the signing a man walked in and laid a stack of papers in front of me. When I started to sign them, he said, "I don't want your autograph. Those are for you. You need to call me." He turned and walked away.

"Okay," I said, puzzled, and I went back to signing autographs.

When the session was finished, I looked at the papers. They were citations from the Colorado Division of Wildlife. I had been charged with harassment of wildlife and illegally taking or having possession of an elk.

A wildlife district manager named Robert Thompson, who took his job way too seriously, told my reporter friend Mr. Lipsher, "I'd like to hear Mr. Murray's side of the story. We have pictures of him sitting on top of, or to the side of, a cow elk that is lying down. I had anonymous informants tell me they were bulldogging elk during that time frame."

I hoped Mr. Thompson didn't pay those informants very much. I would have told him exactly what we'd done if he had asked. He went on to call my actions "troubling" and said, "Getting through the winter is stressful enough for these animals."

Of course Lipsher wrote it all in the *Denver Post* under the juicy banner headline "Cowboy Rodeo Champ Gets Ticket: Did rodeo cowboy star ride elk?"

Yes, I did. I paid a fine for the citations, which cost less than many of the "troubling" speeding tickets I'd gotten in my life. But the story refused to die. Eight years after our snowy romp through that Colorado meadow, I was in a deposition for a lawsuit being filed against the PBR (Professional Bull Riders), a sports franchise I'm a partner in. The lawyer, a credit to his profession, tried to dig up anything and everything on those of us being deposed. When he came to me, he asked, "Mr. Murray, have you ever been in trouble with the Colorado Division of Wildlife?"

"Yeah. I bulldogged an elk."

"You what?"

"I bulldogged an elk." If that clarified things for the counselor, he didn't show it. "You know what steer wrestling is? Well, that's known as bulldogging. I did that to an elk."

After jotting a few worthless notes in his pad, the lawyer said, "Are you proud of that, Mr. Murray?"

"Hell, yes, I'm proud of it. How many people do you know who have bulldogged an elk?"

That's going to be a helluva story for the grandkids. Little could I have known that the Denver ticketing episode was just a prelude.

A lot was in store for me in 1995. By the end of the year the elk citation and the publicity that followed it was the least of my concerns.

7

The Rehab King

I RODE IN fewer rodeos in 1994 than at any other time in my career, seventy-seven, and I earned a moderate $83,613 at the NFR. Still, I won the all-around title by a mile with over $240,000 in earnings. By competing in fewer rodeos, I was fresher and healthier each time I rode, which meant I made better rides.

We also scheduled better in 1994 than ever before. Cody broke his leg at Houston early in the year, so he was sitting at home in his office every day studying the calendar. He says it was his best year ever for scheduling.

This was good, because five straight years of hard traveling and riding, competing in the three toughest rodeo events week in and week out, can take a toll on your body. I had been fortunate that individual injuries had been minimal, but the effects roughstock riding has on your body are cumulative. It's like being in a twenty-mile-an-hour fender bender. Most times you can walk away unhurt. But if you have a hundred of those twenty-mile-an-hour wrecks a year, your body eventually goes on strike.

I'd been riding on a bum knee my entire professional career. During my second year of college, I partially tore the anterior cruciate ligament (ACL) in my left knee while bull-dogging. The ACL is one of the crisscrossing ligaments behind the kneecap that connects the back of the femur (or thighbone) to the front of the tibia (or shinbone). The ACL keeps your shinbone from moving too far forward in relation to your thighbone. I'm not a doctor, but all athletes know about the ACL. It's the most commonly injured ligament among athletes, and it's the injury they dread the most. If you've ever heard a football or basketball player talk about having "a knee," they're referring to a torn ACL. It's normally a season-ender, and in some cases it can end an athlete's career.

Back in college, I'd been lucky. I'd had what medical experts call a "grade two" ACL, which means the ligament was partially torn. I could still walk, ride, even run. I was young and healthy. Foolishly, I never wore a knee brace (if I had to do it over again, I'd never climb on a bull or a bucking horse without knee braces).

Even with a partially blown-out left knee, I rode five full years without any problems. All that changed in August of 1991.

Jim Sharp and I were on our way back home from a rodeo when we decided to stop at our old stomping grounds in Odessa for a charity bull ride at a place called Dos Amigos. The charity was worthwhile, and Jim and I had no problem showing up for the event, but our motivations weren't completely altruistic. Dos Amigos was a wide-open place, a good-time honky-tonk where the beer was cold, the music loud, and the girls pretty. Jerry Jeff Walker played there quite a bit, as did several other famous Texas musicians. The party sometimes spilled outdoors to the small arena Dos Amigos owners had built out back. On this day, the crowd hooted and hollered and cheered for Jim and me as we tried to put on the best show we could for a good cause.

The bulls weren't the rankest of the year, but they were still pretty good. Jim made a good ride, and I followed him with what I thought was a close-to-perfect bull ride. When the whistle blew, I stepped off perfectly. But when I hit the ground, I heard a pop. It sounded like a small-caliber pistol or a firecracker, but I knew it was neither.

My left knee buckled underneath me, and I hit the ground. The ACL I'd injured five years earlier had finally snapped.

At first I was surprised that I could put pressure on my leg. I'd always assumed a torn ligament in your knee crippled you right then and there. My knee was weak, and it bent in ways that were gross to look at, but I could limp along without too much trouble. Then the swelling started. Within an hour of my accident my knee looked like a cantaloupe. "I think I've got a problem," I said to Jim.

"Yeah," he said when he looked at my knee. "You do."

To my surprise, Dr. Tandy Freeman said surgery wasn't necessary. "The laxity is minimal," he said. "I think nonoperative management is an option if you want to go that route."

"Non what?"

"Rehab. The tendon won't heal itself, but at your age if you rehab it, you can continue to ride. There'll come a time when we have to fix it surgically, but that's not something we have to do right this minute if you're not ready."

I wasn't ready. I was leading the all-around standings with less than one hundred days to go in the season. Faced with the option of having surgery and being out for the year, or rehabbing the knee and riding with a brace and a little pain, well, the choice was easy.

Tandy prescribed exercises for my hamstring and quadriceps as well as some flexibility drills. He also suggested a brace that would keep my knee from hyperextending any further.

Three weeks later I was back out, winning the bronc riding at the Original Coors Rodeo Showdown in Scottsdale, Arizona. I scored a 78 on a rank bronc named Copenhagen Bonnie and couldn't have been happier.

"This was the first time I've ridden since getting hurt," I told a local reporter. "I'm happy about how it went. Once I got in the chute, I didn't think about my knee. I just went for it."

I took that same approach with me to the 1994 NFR, but things there didn't go as well as I'd hoped. I rode thirty-one different bucking animals in that ten-day stretch in Las Vegas, but I was bucked off three saddle broncs, and six bulls. I'd been leading the bull riding standings going into the week, but I only managed to make a score in four rounds. If it hadn't been for a second-place finish on the final day, I would have been shut out.

My bareback performance was a lot better. I moved from eleventh place at the start of the event to sixth, and I moved up from eleventh to ninth in the saddle bronc riding.

I won the all-around, but I wished I could have brought home my second bull riding title. "I'm a little disappointed," I said afterward. "But I'm still happy. I get to compete with my friends and have a good time."

Then I added something that would prove prophetic in the coming months: "Rodeo teaches you a lot. It teaches you not to sweat the small stuff."

I STILL RODE with my left knee in a brace at the start of the 1995 season, but I didn't let that slow me down. I had a chance to do something nobody else in history had ever done: win seven all-around world championships.

The season got off to a great start. Once again I found myself in the early all-around and bull riding lead. I could bolster that lead in Fort Worth in February. I was riding well, and I loved the Fort Worth rodeo because it was close to my house. It's always easier to ride when you're sleeping in your own bed, eating your own food, and watching your own TV.

I drew a bull called Night Train. Climbing over the chute, I did exactly what I'd always done, standing on the slats with my feet parallel to the boards, tightening my bull rope, and sliding forward toward my riding hand. I nodded for the chute to open.

The bull hesitated as the gate opened. When he moved, he shot down the length of the gate, hanging my foot in one of the slats. The bull leaped out of the chute, but my leg stayed back in the gate. My knee was pulled in a direction God never intended when he designed that joint. I knew immediately that I'd torn something in my right knee.

This time it was the PCL (posterior cruciate ligament), the other ligament that crisscrosses behind the kneecap. This one keeps the tibia from moving too far backward in relation to the femur. PCL injuries aren't rare, but they aren't as common as torn ACLs. The most common PCL tears occur in car crashes when your knees hit the dashboard. You can also tear the PCL if your knee is locked and somebody hits you in the kneecap. Somehow my leg was pulled in just the right way to partially tear my PCL.

Fortunately it wasn't a total tear. I could still walk (something I wouldn't have been able to do if the PCL had snapped completely), so I went on about my business.

At least I wouldn't be favoring my left knee, I thought. Now they were both bum.

I never complained to Tandy about my right knee

because it never hurt the way my left one did. Perhaps it was the age of the injury—the left knee had developed a lot of wear and tear due to continued use with a torn ligament—or that the right knee tear wasn't severe enough to cause me a great deal of pain. Either way, when Tandy was checking me out in March of 1995, I never mentioned my right knee to him.

Later that year it was all the two of us talked about.

In late March, I went to the PBR Bud Light Cup event in Rancho Marietta, California, a weekend-long professional bull riding event that pitted the best bull riders against the best bulls. I drew a big white bull named Butterfly owned by Dan Russell. This was a tough draw, but none of the bulls in the PBR were duds.

Again I prepared for my ride as I always did: nothing unusual or out of the ordinary. PBR events are a little showier than your average PRCA rodeo because the bull riders cater to a broader televised audience, and PBR events are compressed into two nights rather than ten days. But the arena is still the arena and the bulls are still rank. I had walked out under the pyrotechnics and strobe lights during the introductions like every other cowboy, but once I climbed into the chute, this was just another bull ride.

The chute opened and I reacted as Butterfly jumped forward and kicked. He spun to his right into my riding arm, so I adjusted my weight and used my legs to stay centered on him.

Then I felt my knee explode. I don't know if I heard it

as much as felt it, but the snap and pop were unmistakable. At least one ligament in my right knee was gone.

The pain was overwhelming. I had to glance down to make sure my leg was still there. What I saw shocked me. It was like my knee was a universal joint and my leg was a rag-doll attachment stuck onto my body with glue. It was as though my skin was the only thing holding my lower leg and foot to the rest of my body. I wanted to vomit. But I had another problem. The bull was still bucking. I was in the middle of a ride. It seemed easier to stay on him than to get off.

I had to finish my ride one-legged, which I did. Once the whistle blew, I used the bull's momentum to step off and throw myself clear of his path. I hit the ground on my left leg (the one in a brace that I'd screwed up years earlier) and scooted out of the bull's path as best I could. Then I went down.

Tandy was behind the chutes that night, as he is for every PBR event, so I knew I was in good hands medically even though I was hurting like I'd never hurt before. "Uh-oh," he said when he looked at my leg.

"What is it?" I asked.

"We'll have to get X rays to confirm, but it looks like you've torn your posterior cruciate ligament."

"I don't know what I've torn, but it hurts like hell whatever it is."

I could see from the look on Tandy's face that this was not a two-weeks-and-you're-back kind of injury. "It's going to be all right," he said to me. But I knew it wasn't.

To put things in perspective,
the gate is six feet tall, and Perfect Storm, the bull,
weighs about 1,800 pounds. *(Allen Glanville)*

Me and Dad fishing at the ranch. *(Murray family)*

Hugging my mom
good-bye as I'm boarding
a private jet on my way
to another rodeo.
(Murray family)

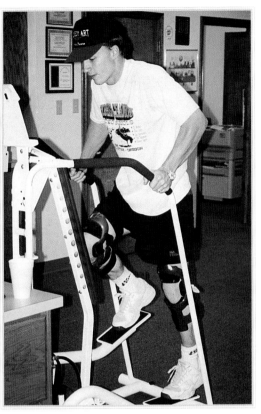

Rehabbing two bad knees.
(Kendra Santos)

Trying to take the term "all-around cowboy"
to a new level. *(Murray family)*

There's no greater rush in the world than the moment that chute opens.
I won this particular battle with Yellow One in 1999. *(Allen Glanville)*

Stretching has always been part of my pre-ride ritual.
Here I am at the 2002 PBR Finals. *(Shari Van Alsburg)*

The Hard Copy ride. *(Susan Lambeth)*

Saddle bronc riding is about timing and technical proficiency.
(PRCA photo by Mike Copeman)

Me and Mom moments
after I had won my seventh all-around
world title in 1998. *(Susan Lambeth)*

Me and Larry Mahan, after I broke Larry's record
of six All-Around Cowboy titles.
Who looks happier? *(Kendra Santos)*

A rough bunch if there ever was one: Cody, me, Jewel, and Jim Sharp taking a break from branding calves in west Texas. *(Murray family)*

Later that night I was lying on a cot in the on-site medical center behind the locker rooms. It was really a glorified tent, although it housed every first-aid supply the doctors and medical staff might need. The only supply I cared about, however, was the pillow under my head. The injury was bad, not just hurting-like-hell kind of bad, but long-term, out-of-commission, potential-career-ending bad. I'd seen football players who never came back from injuries that looked a lot milder than this. It was too early to jump to any conclusions, I knew, but that didn't stop my mind from sprinting through all the worst-case scenarios. As I stared at the top of the tent, I couldn't help wondering if I'd ridden my last bull.

Then I heard a small voice. "Mr. Murray . . . Mr. Murray." It was a kid's voice, coming from outside a small crack in the tent no more than a foot from my cot. "Mr. Murray, can you sign my poster? Hey, Mr. Murray."

I closed my eyes and pretended I didn't hear him.

"Mr. Murray . . . Mr. Murray."

This was fitting, I thought. Here I was lying on my back after the worst injury of my career, an injury I couldn't even figure out—I hadn't wrecked and had scored pretty decent on the bull!—and this kid wanted an autograph. The PBR had given out posters of me to kids as a promotion before the event, so I knew what he wanted me to sign.

What I didn't expect was to be whacked on the head. "Mr. Murray . . . Mr. Murray." Thwack! "Mr. Murray." Thwack. Thwack. Thwack.

It took me a second to realize the kid had reached

through the crack in the tent and was hitting me in the head with a rolled-up poster. This was just what I needed. Insult piled high on top of injury. Here I was struggling through pain, doubt, anger, every emotion that accompanies a serious injury, and this kid was hitting me in the head with a poster of *me*.

What could possibly come next?

THE ANSWER TO that question came the very next day. Invasive surgery is the only course of treatment for a snapped PCL, but you can't go under the knife immediately. The swelling can be severe and long-term. Before a surgeon can go in and effect any repairs, that swelling has to go down.

I hobbled around on crutches for two months waiting for the leg to return to its normal size so Tandy could cut open my knee and, hopefully, repair the damage. Even then there were no guarantees. PCL reconstruction is rarer and trickier than ACL surgery. The procedure is lengthy and difficult, and the results are less predictable. At the time there was no way to know whether my career was over. All I could do was sit around and wait for my mammoth knee to shrink.

It was the most helpless feeling in the world.

On June 30, Tandy opened up my right knee and repaired my torn PCL, taking material from the middle third of my patellar tendon to rebuild the ligament, then reattaching it to the bone.

When I woke up after surgery, I couldn't feel my legs. I was groggy from the anesthesia, but not so out of it that I didn't feel a wave of panic rush over me. I couldn't move my leg or my feet, and when I reached down and pinched myself below the waist, I didn't feel a thing.

Mom and Dad were in the room with me. "Get the nurse!" I shouted. When the nurse arrived, I said, "Where's Tandy? I need to talk to him right now."

"He'll be in to check on you tomorrow," she said.

"No," I said, the panic rising in my voice. "I need to talk to him right now."

Tandy was much more than a good surgeon; he was a great friend. I knew his pager number by heart, so when I got nowhere with the nursing staff, I picked up the phone and paged him. He was back at the hospital and at my side within the hour.

"Don't panic, everything went fine," he said.

"Like hell it did. I can't feel my leg." I didn't want this to be a "There, there, you're paralyzed but at least we saved the leg" sort of speech.

"I know," Tandy said. "The procedure was so long that it stopped all circulation in your leg. It'll take a couple more hours before you regain any feeling. But you're fine. Now, we just have to watch closely for infection and get you on a program of exercise and rehab."

"How long will I be out?"

"Normal recovery time is about nine months."

Nine months. A full season. I would miss the NFR, the PBR Bud Light Cup Finals, and all the rodeos where I was defending all-around champion. There would be no seventh consecutive all-around world title, no record-breaking celebrations, no more rides. For the better part of a year, I was done.

"If I'm going to be out anyway, why don't we go ahead and repair my other knee," I said.

Tandy agreed. The ACL recovery time was about six months, and it would be another two months before we could schedule the surgery. If I was going to be laid up anyway, I might as well get both those problems corrected at the same time.

In mid-September I had surgery to repair my torn left ACL. Both operations went well. There were no complications or infections, no surprises or other damage that Tandy didn't already know about. If I'd been an accountant or banker, everything would have been great. I'd have been back at work in no time. But as a rodeo cowboy I knew I had a lot of work ahead.

My knees had been repaired. Now it was up to me to get them ready to ride.

THE TWO WEEKS of the 1995 NFR were the toughest I'd gone through in a while. Calf roper Joe Beaver won the all-around title, his first. I couldn't have been happier for Joe, but watching him take the buckle I'd held for six straight years was tough, especially given the circumstances.

ESPN asked me to provide on-air color commentary, which I did, but there was an emptiness to the whole event for me. I couldn't be out there in the chutes, I knew that, but the road from knowing something in your head to accepting it in your gut can be a long one. I hated being a spectator. I would have worked twenty-four hours a day if I had thought it would have sped up the process and gotten me back in the NFR as a competitor.

If missing the NFR wasn't motivation enough, a lot of guys were writing me off, convinced that my surgeries, while not career-ending, were at least career-altering. They said I'd never be the same even if I did come back.

One incident in particular hammered that message home. In between my two surgeries, my agent, Tony Garritano, got a call from a marketing executive at Bud Light, one of the sponsors with whom I'd developed a great relationship.

"We're reevaluating our strategies, and we're going to go a different route," the exec said.

"Why?" Tony asked.

"Well, various reasons. This is part of an overall strategic reevaluation. Plus, with Ty's knees and the surgeries, quite frankly we think he's done."

Done. Written off. After six years of being the most

dominant rodeo cowboy in the world, and one of the most loyal and hardworking corporate spokesmen in all of sports, I was now expendable, damaged, and in the words of Bud Light, "done."

It's not like I expected any company to keep me around out of the goodness of their collective hearts. Business is business. But to shuck me aside like a bad ear of corn because of one injury was a little much. If I'd tried to come back and hadn't made it, or if I'd somehow decided that my heart wasn't into riding anymore, then I could have understood their position.

I still had stitches in my knee, and people were assuming I was finished. That hurt. It also drove me to get back out there and prove to the world that I was far from "done." I'd lived my whole life with the goal of breaking Larry Mahan's six-time world champion record. The injuries to my knees interrupted that goal, but that didn't alter my resolve.

I was coming back. It was just a matter of time.

THE DARK CLOUD of injury had one silver lining. The layoff gave me time to catch up on life. I spent time with friends and family and finally fulfilled one of my lifelong dreams by buying a two-thousand-acre ranch in Stephenville, Texas. It had been a working ranch with two houses and a bunkhouse, several ponds and fishing holes, a beautiful stream, and plenty of woods, fields, and wildlife. It was the perfect place to raise cattle and horses.

In my first year of ownership I built an arena and a small one-room cabin in the center of the ranch along the bank of the stream, a place with no electricity or running water, heated by an old wood-burning stove and lit by the flame of a lantern. I spent hours in that little cabin, away from phones, faxes, televisions, radios, not even the hum of a lightbulb or the whir of a refrigerator motor to distract me. The only sounds were the songs of birds, water running over rocks in the stream, and the slow patter of hooves as deer walked past looking for food.

That connecting with nature, with the simple life the way things were a century ago, was something I had missed while I was working the whirlwind rodeo schedule. Finding it again at my cabin made me realize how much I'd lost, and how important it was never to lose it again. I vowed to spend more time away, out in the woods fishing and camping and being around wildlife, which I did throughout the rest of my career. Whether it was taking a few days between rodeos to go camping in the mountains, or retreating to the cabin on my ranch for a weekend, I never again lost that connection to the simpler life.

Later in my career I chose to escape for a few days, after a PBR event in Reno, to the Sierras with my girl-friend, Jewel, and Pat Russell, an old California rancher and dear friend of mine. We camped and fished and enjoyed the beauty of one of the most magnificent places on earth.

When we drove down from the mountains, we noticed a flag at half-staff outside a small post office. "Wonder what happened?" my girlfriend asked.

"Postmaster must have died or something," I said.

Then we noticed another flag lowered outside a school, then house after house with small American flags in the yards. "I don't think this is for a postmaster," my girlfriend said.

Not until we reached Reno did we learn what had happened. The date was September 13, 2001.

I LOVED THE RANCH and everything it represented. After years of working my ass off, I had finally been able to buy my own little slice of heaven. Thanks to my injury I now had time to enjoy it.

But I wasn't ready to kick back and relax too long, and when the 1996 season rolled around, I was itching to get back out and ride.

Denver was another rodeo I hated missing. It was always the first big one of the year, the official launch of the cowboy's season, and no roughstock rider wanted to miss it. Unfortunately, I didn't have a choice. The knees were coming along, but I wasn't there yet. I'd gone through weight training, flexibility drills, assisted stretches where I thought the trainer was going to pull my legs off, as well as heat, ice, and electronic stimulation, but it was a slow process.

There wasn't one aspect of the knee I didn't know as well as any first-year medical student. I climbed one hundred flights of stairs a day on the stair machine and ran on the treadmill until I was dripping with sweat. Every time I'd think I needed a break, I'd ask myself, "How bad do you want it? You done, or are you coming back?" With each added step I had my answer.

I RETURNED TO competition in March of 1996, better than ever, or so I thought. For six weeks it looked like I was back at the top of my game. Then in Del Rio, Texas, I had another strange incident during a bull ride.

The bull, named Bad Moon, was one of the ranker bulls in the herd. Having made it to the short round at the George Paul Memorial Bull Riding, I was looking forward to the challenge. After a year on the sidelines, I couldn't wait for every ride.

The chute opened and Bad Moon started spinning. He was turning back into my riding hand while I was a little bit out of position, leaning too far to my left for the momentum the bull was carrying into the turn. I lifted my free hand above and behind my head to counterbalance the momentum of the bull, and to get myself back into position in the middle of him. When I made that move, the bull kicked and I went back on him.

That's when I felt a pop in my shoulder, the kind of

crack you might feel if you accidentally ran into the corner of a wall or the sharp edge of a piece of furniture. I didn't think anything about it. In fact, I scored 84 on Bad Moon that night and finished second, another good showing in what I hoped would be a comeback year.

The next week I traveled to the PBR event in Charlotte, North Carolina, where I rode well enough to split the win with Jim Sharp. We were no longer roommates, but we remained great friends, so it felt good to share my first return bull-riding victory with an old friend who'd watched me struggling through rehab. But I had a niggling sense of anxiety about the win. My shoulder continued to hurt, even when I was just walking around. That wasn't natural or normal. Usually the pain in a sore shoulder went away after a day or two. This pain, however, was getting progressively worse.

I dreaded telling Tandy about the pain for fear of hearing more bad news, but I didn't have any choice. Two weeks after I felt that initial pop, I could barely move my arm. Any attempt to raise my free hand above my head was like sticking a knife in my deltoid and twisting it. He ordered a series of X rays and scans; when he came into the office to give me the news, I had my answer from the expression on his face.

"You have a subluxation of the left shoulder," he said.

"A what?"

"A dislocated shoulder."

"Okay. Let's pop it back in."

He was shaking his head before I finished. "That's a shoulder separation. A dislocated shoulder is something a lot different, a lot worse unfortunately. You've pulled a ligament called the labrum, which is what the cartilage is attached to in order to hold your shoulder bone in the socket. Because the labrum has been pulled away from the bone, your shoulder slipped partially out of the socket. Even if it were to pop back in, there's no ligament to hold it in place."

I hung my head knowing what was coming next. "Surgery?"

"Yep. We have to go in from the front of your shoulder and reattach the ligament to the bone. It's a pretty big operation."

"How long?"

"Normal recovery time is about six months."

Six more months. Another season. If everything went great, no complications, no infections, perfect rehab, I would be back in November, too late to compete in any meaningful rodeos and far too late to qualify for any season-ending finals. I was out for another year.

BY NOW I was feeling like the rehab king. I'd been in physical therapy for a year working on strengthening my knees and getting my lower body back in shape. Now I had to start the process over again, only this time it was the shoulder I needed to rehab. I was twenty-six years old and embarking on my second straight year of painstaking, methodical treatment just to get back to where I was when I was twenty-four. To call it frustrating would be an understatement.

Fortunately, I never let my frustration turn negative. I never pouted or sang the blues. I guess that's just part of growing up a cowboy. You learn to take what life throws your way and handle it the best way you know how. Cody had broken his leg, his jaw, and sprained every joint in his body, but he never once bitched about it. He just took what the sport gave him and moved on. Jim had been sidelined with knee injuries in 1993 and 1994 and had made only a limited comeback in 1995, but he had never uttered a word of complaint. He just worked to fix the problems and come back. I knew I had to do the same.

In my case, that meant learning the intricacies of shoulder anatomy, slowly working to reacquire a full range of motion, then rebuilding strength and stamina in an arm that was critical for me to compete as a roughstock rider. I didn't like being hurt, but I could do nothing about it. My choices were to sit around and say "Woe is me" or press ahead and do whatever it took to get back to riding.

At first I couldn't raise my arm chest high. I couldn't pick up a coffee cup or open a truck door. Anything that required two hands—from pushing a lawn mower to opening a jar of mayonnaise—was out of the question. I couldn't even put deodorant under my right arm because it required me to use my left. When little things like putting your hand flat on a table then lifting it six inches off the surface for five or six seconds were so painful and exhausting, it took hours and sometimes days to complete one task.

Slowly, though, I began to see progress. My shoulder got stronger as the weeks passed, and my range of motion steadily improved. One morning I was happy to discover I could actually open one of the cabinets above my stove. Then I realized I could reach into the refrigerator and pull out a half gallon of milk. It wasn't easy. A box of raisin bran felt like an anvil for several weeks, but I could sense I was making progress.

I also worked with enough rubber bands to open a Goodyear dealership, pulling the straps up and out to work my deltoid and rotator cuff. The pain I experienced with those exercises sometimes made me want to cry. But I pulled and lifted, stretched and pushed every muscle, tendon, and ligament in my shoulder until it was not only back to normal, it was stronger than it had ever been. All summer I exercised, never missing a day of rehab.

By the fall I was enjoying the ranch, putting up hay and looking after my cattle, and putting the finishing touches on my little cabin while making a few changes to the big house. When November came around, Tandy released me to ride. The only problem was there was nothing to ride in. The season was effectively over.

I would make my return in January in Denver. It was as good a place as any, a big rodeo to kick off a fresh start in a fresh year. I was ready. Nineteen ninety-seven was going to be my year.

• • •

I CAME OUT blazing. I felt equally strong in all three events, and I was having more fun riding than I'd had in a long time. I had always heard that you sometimes have to be away from the things you love to truly appreciate them. That was literally true in my case. Being away from rodeo for two years made me enjoy my return more than I'd enjoyed riding since I was a kid. I'd always loved it, but at times I'd looked at it like a job, when I was sore and tired and lacked the childlike enthusiasm that had made riding so special for me. Now that euphoria was back. I was like a kid at Christmas, back in the arena where I belonged, having more fun than a grown man ought to be allowed to have.

Denver was as big and as loud as ever. I was back, and feeling great. Then in Fort Worth, I won the all-around title and had one of the best bareback rides I'd had in a long time on a horse called Wild West. "I'm going full blast," I told a reporter after the Fort Worth event. "My whole body feels really good. I'm ready for the rest of the year."

Little could I have known how short my season would be.

ON FEBRUARY 8, 1997, one week after winning the all-around title in Fort Worth, I climbed on a bull called Bar Fly at the PBR Bud Light Cup event in St. Louis. I felt good about my bull riding going into the week. When the chute opened, I thought everything was good.

But the bull turned back away from my hand, pulling me out of position. I tried to use my legs and free arm to get back in the middle, but it was too late. My center of gravity was too far over and the bull's momentum was throwing me off and to the right. I made one last-ditch effort to recover, but it was no use. Bar Fly threw me high in the air and I was coming down back first.

I fell quickly, too quickly to turn over and brace myself. I was going onto my right side, so my reflexes took over. I braced myself with my right elbow, driving it into the dirt to break my fall. When my elbow hit the ground, I heard another sickening pop. This time I felt the ligaments of my right shoulder tear, and I felt the ball of my right shoulder pop out of its socket.

It had happened again! One month into my comeback after a two-year absence, I had dislocated (not separated) my shoulder. This time it was my right shoulder, my riding arm, the one I needed to hold on to the stock I was riding. As I was flopping around in the dirt of the St. Louis arena, pain swelled up in me so quickly that I thought I was going to pass out, vomit, or both.

I also thought about all the hard work I'd gone through to get back to this point. Now, if my self-diagnosis was correct (and I had no doubt that it was), I was looking at another year of surgery and rehab. Another season lost. Another chance at breaking the record gone in the blink of an eye.

It took Tandy forty minutes to get my shoulder back into place. He put his foot on my ribs and pulled my arm as hard as he could, but my muscles had locked up because of the trauma. His staff had to shoot me full of morphine and Valium to relax the muscles enough to get my shoulder back in place. I begged Tandy to either kill the pain or kill me, and I didn't care which he chose. Bile rose up in my throat as the pain intensified. "Just cut the damn thing off," I said at least once. Amputation couldn't hurt any worse.

It wasn't until much later that I thought about the long term. Two years before, Bud Light had said I was "done," a comment that wasn't meant to be mean-spirited, but one I had used to motivate me, to drive me to run that one extra mile or to climb that one extra flight of stairs, or to pull that god-awful rubber band another hundred times. Now, after all that work, I had just sustained another season-ending injury. I had another round of surgery, another stint in rehab, and another birthday to look forward to, all before I ever climbed onto another bull or bucking horse.

How many others would doubt that I would ever come back?

8

The Program

I TRIED TO PUT a happy face on my situation. "The fact is this is a dangerous sport," I wrote in a column for *Wrangler* magazine. "I was really excited about being back, and it's darn sure discouraging that after seven injury-free years I'm having three in a row go like this. I could sit around and pout about it, but that won't fix my shoulder. But I'll be back. I'm a cowboy. That is what I do."

I was hurt, mad, frustrated, depressed, and determined all at the same time. After every injury I believed I would come back, but this one had me questioning myself. Was I getting too old? Hell, I wasn't even close to thirty yet! How could my body become injury-prone at this age? Was I doing something wrong that was causing me to get injured? You might suspect that without knowing the circumstances of each injury, but I had lived through them all so I knew they weren't my fault. They were flukes, every one of them.

The injuries roughstock riders sustain are not too different from those of NFL players—concussions being the most common, followed by broken bones, and knee injuries. Shoulder separations are fourth or fifth on our list, but just like in football, they are devastating. You rarely see quarterbacks come back from this kind of injury, and you'd be hard-pressed to find a running back who has ever been the same after ACL and PCL surgery. I had endured it all: two blown-out knees and now two dislocated shoulders. If I'd been an NFL player, the pundits would have written me off and sent me packing.

As positive as I tried to remain, I couldn't stop those thoughts from creeping into my head, especially at night as I was lying awake in my bed trying to get comfortable enough to catch an hour or two of sleep. Because of the swelling I again had to wait almost four weeks before Tandy could perform the surgery. During that time my arm was wrapped against my body in a sling. Anytime I rolled onto my right side, pain ran through me like a gunshot, and I would sit up in a jolt. Sleep came in fits and starts and I became irritable as the hours of deprivation piled up. Those were the times when I questioned myself the most. Why was this happening? Why had I had three year-ending injuries in a row? When would I be back? And when I did get back, would I still be at the top of my game?

The surgery came on March 3, 1997, and Tandy declared it a success. "You have more damage this time," he said, giving me news I already knew. "The rotator cuff will require more work to rehab, and it'll take a little longer to regain a full range of motion. Fortunately, you won't need as much range since it's your riding arm, but you'll have to work on getting your strength back."

"How long?" I asked.

"Six to nine months, same as last time."

I closed my eyes and nodded. It was what I'd expected. Another nine months of rehab. Another season gone.

I SENSED A CHANGE in the way people looked at me after the fourth surgery. I couldn't think of a single top-ranked athlete who had come back from two knee and two shoulder surgeries, and I sure as heck couldn't remember anybody doing it and regaining his old form. Joe Namath had more knee operations, but he never won a second Super Bowl. John Smoltz had similar shoulder surgery and came back strong as a relief pitcher, but he was never the dominant starter he had once been. Dominique Wilkins, Garrison Hearst, the list went on and on.

Fortunately my parents and close friends never questioned my future. Mom and Dad would always preface everything they said with "when you get back," as in "When you get back, we'll have to come up to Denver and see you" or "When you get back, we'll check the schedule and see if we can't come to Fort Worth." There was never an *if* or a *maybe* from them. The question was already answered in their minds: I would definitely be back.

The big questions were when would I be back and what kind of shape would I be in when I made my return. I'd busted my butt in rehab after my knee surgeries, logging more miles on the treadmill than a lot of marathon runners, and lifting more leg weights than some professional bodybuilders. When I'd come back, my knees and legs were as strong as they had ever been. Then I messed up my shoulder. So I spent a year doing nothing but building up my front, center, and rear deltoids, redeveloping my rhomboidei and trapeziuses, and stretching my rotator cuff. When I came back, my left shoulder was as strong and flexible as it had ever been. But my right shoulder wasn't ready for the impact of that one fateful fall. It seemed that when I fixed one problem, another body part went bad.

Maybe that was the problem. Maybe I had been approaching the whole rehab process with the wrong mind-set. Maybe I'd been focusing too much on rebuilding the injured areas of my body and not enough on keeping my entire body in shape for riding.

I had plenty of time to ponder this theory as my shoulder slowly healed enough for me to begin exercising. At first I started working on raising my arm to chest height, then shoulder height, then lifting my arm over my head, just as I'd done the year before with my left arm. By now I knew the drill. I'd progress to light weights, then heavier lifting coupled with stretching and massage therapy. Resistance training would come later, as would the speed and agility drills. I was the Rehab King. I knew all the procedures.

But maybe those very procedures had got me into this injury cycle in the first place. After knee surgery I'd focused on my knees and let the rest of my body go. The same was true after my first shoulder surgery. My shoulder came back in great shape, but I'd essentially ignored the rest of my body during rehab. Not that I was ever in bad shape—I worked hard at remaining physically fit during all my stints in rehab—but I wasn't in riding shape. That stint from 1995 when I hurt my knee until my return in 1996 was the first time in my life I'd gone a year without riding. The longest stint I'd gone before that was a month at the most, and it had been years since I'd taken that much time off.

Sure I was in good shape when I returned, but I wasn't in riding shape. It's like an NFL player after training camp. He might be in the best shape of his life, but he's not really in game shape until he gets a few weeks of full contact under his belt. I was in pretty good shape when I came back from my surgeries, and my injured parts were stronger than they had ever been, but I didn't have the total package.

With that in mind, I set out on a new course of action. This time around I was going to rehab the injury, but I was also going to retrain my entire body. I was going to get myself in not just good shape but iron man kind of shape, the best shape of my life. Without actually riding, I was going to get myself as close to riding shape as possible.

The only question was, how?

MY ANSWER CAME during a casual conversation with Jim Sharp. I told Jim I was looking for a good trainer near home and asked him if he knew anybody. "You should go see the guy that's teaching me karate," he said.

"I don't want to learn karate. I'm looking for a trainer."

"I'm telling you, this is your guy. He's the most kick-ass trainer I've ever seen in my life. If you go to him, you better be ready. He will work you into the ground."

I was ready, and this sounded like the kind of guy I'd be interested in talking to. "What's his name?" I asked Jim.

"Jesse Marquez Lomalli."

WITHIN A COUPLE of days I had a meeting set up with Jesse in his Stephenville karate studio. As far as curb appeal, the place didn't look like much. The dojo was in a low-rise shopping center next door to a lumber store. When I walked through the glass door, the first thing I saw was an insurance office and a nail salon. The dojo was in the back, down a dark concrete hallway that could have used a good scrubbing. When I opened the door, the first thing I noticed was the heat. It felt like a sauna in there. The guy's air-conditioning must have been broken, which had to be terrible for business.

The walls of the outer office were filled with photos, and the shelves just below the ceiling were littered with trophies. Jesse must have been quite the competitor, or so I gathered from the pictures and awards. One picture showed a fireplug of a man I assumed to be Jesse breaking a baseball bat with his shin. Just looking at that one made me wince. The few times I'd bumped my shins on the bedpost I'd hobbled around and cussed up a storm. This guy broke bats with his. Then I saw a shot of him in midkick, with one leg fully extended and the other tucked beneath him like a leaping panther. But I wasn't astonished by the kick itself as much as the background. A man was standing right behind Jesse in the photo. I had no idea how tall that man was, but Jesse had jumped a good six inches higher than the man's head. Even if the guy in the background was a dwarf, Jesse had a pretty impressive vertical leap.

Then I saw a poster taped haphazardly to what appeared to be the door to an industrial freezer. The poster showed a close-up of a man's face grimacing with anguish, sweat pouring off his forehead, as he clenched his teeth. There was no doubt that this guy was hurting. The caption below the photo read, "Pain Is Good." At that moment I had a feeling Jim was right: this Jesse fellow appeared to be serious.

"Are you Ty?" I heard a voice from behind me.

"Yeah." I turned around and saw that the man in the photographs was, indeed, Jesse Marquez Lomalli. He was shorter and stockier than I'd expected. My first-blush guess put him at about five feet eight inches, and about two hundred pounds of solid muscle. His neck wasn't a neck at all, just a hunk of muscle running from his earlobes to his shoulders, which were themselves the size of boxing gloves. His chest was thick and barreled, but there didn't appear to be a lot of taper down to his waist. He looked like a power lifter, stocky from his neck to his knees. "You must be Jesse," I said, extending my hand.

"That's right. The coolest, the badest, the Shogun of Stephenville."

I'm not sure if I flinched when he grabbed my hand, but I was certainly surprised by his grip. It felt like a horse had stepped on my palm. I noticed a smile on his face as he shook my hand, not a nice-to-meet-you smile, but a cold how-do-you-like-that smile. Then he said, "So, you want to get in shape, huh?"

I spent the next fifteen minutes explaining my situation, telling him about my riding and my injuries, the rehab, and my theory about getting myself back into riding shape. "I don't want to learn karate," I said. "I'm not interested in self-defense. What I want to do is hire you to get my entire body in shape, from my hair to my toenails, so that when I come back from this shoulder surgery, I'll be ready to ride."

While I was standing there talking with Jesse, a woman walked in with her son, a boy of probably twelve or thirteen who was carrying far too much weight for his age. "Hello," the mother said, "I'd like to sign my boy up for karate lessons."

"No," Jesse said.

"Excuse me?"

"No. He's too fat."

"Well, I never—"

Jesse interrupted the woman, "You need to put him on a diet and have him run every day. If he loses weight and gets in shape, I'll consider teaching him. Right now, I'd kill him if he came to one of my classes."

The woman grabbed her son by the arm and left in a huff, her heels clicking like the hooves of a stepping horse on the concrete floor.

"Think you were a little tough on her?" I asked.

Jesse laughed. "Man, you haven't seen tough. Earlier this year I got fed up with how out of shape one of my classes was, so I took them out for a five-mile run on the gravel bed of the railroad tracks. That might have been okay, but I made them run barefooted. They were whining and crying, their feet were bleeding, but screw it, I'd had enough of their pansy crap. I didn't ask them to do something I wasn't doing right beside them. I ran every step."

I stood there for a second asking myself the age-old question "What the hell do you say to that?" When I finally gathered myself enough to keep up my end of the conversation, I said, "So, how'd that work out for you?"

"Not too well. I lost about ninety percent of the class that day. I might have overcooked it a little, especially with the women and kids, but to hell with it. If they can't keep up, I don't want them."

I extended my hand again. "Jesse, I think this is going to work out just right."

I HIRED JESSE to train me for two hours a day five days a week for as long as it took to get me ready to ride again. The first things he asked for were tapes of my rides, which surprised me, but I gave them to him. When I asked what he planned to do with them, he said he wanted to study my movements so he could design specific exercises for my riding. That was impressive.

What I didn't realize and couldn't have known at the time was what a psycho Jesse truly was. My first day of training I walked into the dojo and realized that the heavy door looked as if it had come off an industrial freezer for a reason: the dojo was an abandoned meat locker.

When I walked in, I realized that the melting heat I had felt my first day there wasn't because the air-conditioning was broken. There was no air-conditioning. It had to be ninety degrees in there. I noticed an oscillating fan in the corner, so before we got started, I walked over and tried to turn it on. It didn't work. Jesse laughed at me and said, "That's just a prop to make you think about what you're missing." Then the smile faded and he said, "Let's get to work."

We started with what he called "fast-twitch" exercises, little movements he designed to improve my small reflexes. He had me stand straight up and hold my arms straight out in front of me. Then he said, "Make a fist, then open your fingers as many times as you can in ten minutes." The first thirty seconds or so I thought this was silly. How could making a fist and opening my hands get me in shape for riding? A minute later my forearms began to burn and I realized the muscles this exercise was working. Two minutes after that I was slowing down and my forearms felt like lead.

"Come on," Jesse shouted, "just six minutes to go."

Six minutes! I didn't think I could go another six seconds.

"Don't slow down," he said. And I didn't. It helped that Jesse was right beside me doing the exercise with me. I'd trained with coaches who stood on the sidelines and barked instructions without breaking a sweat. You trained harder when your instructor was working right beside you. When the ten minutes were finally up, I felt like my arms were on fire.

"Okay," Jesse said. "Let's get started."

We worked abdominals until I was sure I was going to pass out. Then we started skipping rope. "Left foot only," Jesse shouted, and I hopped on my left foot for a solid minute until I was sure I was going to fall over. "Come on," he said. "Just a hundred and fifty more."

That was when I knew this freak was crazy. There was no way I could skip rope on my left foot for that long. But somehow I did it with Jesse doing every rep right beside me.

When we progressed to the right foot, I thought my left leg was going to fall off at the hip. This time I knew what was coming, so I tried to pace myself.

Jesse was having none of it. "Hop two steps forward," he shouted.

I did as instructed.

"Now take two steps to the right."

I followed orders, assuming this was his way of breaking the monotony.

Then the instructions stopped. I continued to jump, but I noticed that the temperature, which was already stuck somewhere north of ninety degrees, had gone up a notch or two. When I looked up, I realized that Jesse had just moved me underneath the lightbulb.

"Ha, ha, ha! Hot enough for you?" he said.

Yes, it was, but I didn't dare say anything. Not only was he a workout maniac, I felt like this guy had a deep, dark mean streak he would love to show anyone who questioned him. We continued to work nonstop for the entire two hours, no downtime, and no second or two to catch your breath. From the moment I entered the dojo until the moment I staggered out two hours later, we worked as hard as humanly possible.

When I left, I thought I was going to die.

THE NEXT MORNING I felt like I'd been in a wreck. I hurt in places I didn't think you could hurt. The last thing I wanted to do was go back to that deranged sadist. Then I realized that if he had hurt me this bad on the first day, it would have to get better. There was no way we could work any harder than we had on day one. It would have to get easier.

Boy, was I wrong. To my surprise we didn't start the second day with the same exercises we had on day one. This time he had me lie flat on my back and hold my feet straight up above my head.

Jesse stood over me and grabbed my ankles. "Keep your legs straight. I'm going to throw your feet to the ground and you're going to stop them before they hit the floor. Got it?"

"I think so."

He shoved my feet so hard that they bounced when they hit the floor.

"No," he shouted. "Don't be a wuss. I'm going to throw them to the floor and you're going to stop them before they hit. You gonna let me win that easy?"

"Not now." Now that I understood what he was doing, I was sure I could stop my feet before they hit the floor.

The first time I stopped them, it felt like someone had stuck a knife in my lower abdomen. "Get 'em back up here. Quick! Quick! Get 'em up here."

Jesse would have made a great drill instructor on Parris Island. Later I learned that he had lived and studied in Japan, spoke fluent Japanese, and had reached the point in martial arts where it was more of a religion than a sport. In Texas, he'd whipped every martial artist who'd challenged him and a few who hadn't. I didn't know any of that in the first couple of days. All I knew was that he was kicking my butt. I'd been working out since I was thirteen years old and had trained with some of the toughest coaches in sports, but I'd never been through anything like this.

"Get 'em up here, wuss. You gonna let me beat you, wuss? Huh? You giving up?"

I kept my legs straight and threw my feet as hard as I could at his nose. He caught my ankles.

"That's it. Now don't let 'em hit the ground." This time he threw them so hard I thought my heels would punch a hole in the floor, but I caught them an instant before they touched. My lower abs were close to cramping by that point.

"Get 'em up here. Now! Now! Faster, you friggin' wuss! Quick!"

Up my feet went, then back down, then up again. On and on it went, and every time I thought my abs were going to revolt. I began to feel it deep inside as if this exercise were working straight through my stomach and into my back.

"Again!" he shouted. "Get 'em up here."

After fifty or so reps I felt like I was getting accustomed to the routine. Then he changed it.

"Tighten up," he said as he threw my feet down.

I didn't think I could get any tighter, but then just before my feet hit the ground, I felt a crushing blow above my navel.

He had punched me! The sicko had hit me with his fist! How could he do that? And where was all the air that had been in the room just a second ago?

"Get 'em up! Now! Quick! Quick!"

I didn't think I could move after the hammer blow to the gut, but I heaved my legs up one more time, only to have Jesse throw them back down and reward me with another smash to the belly. This new routine went on for a good hundred reps or so. When we finished, I rolled over onto my stomach and tried not to pass out.

"Now we're good and warm," he said. "Let's get after it."

For the next forty minutes we kicked and jumped and did a complex series of calisthenics unlike anything I'd ever seen before. It didn't take me long to figure out that every day was different with Jesse. When I finally finished my sessions with him, I realized I had trained two hours a day, five days a week, for a year and had never done the same thing twice. A few months into the process I nicknamed him the Man of Ten Thousand Exercises.

But on that second day, those sorts of affectionate informalities seemed a long way off. About twenty minutes into our cardio workout I was hurting. My eyes burned, my muscles ached, I couldn't get oxygen into my system fast enough, and to top it all off, it was hot enough in the place to fry an egg. I closed my eyes and gritted my teeth as Jesse continued to count reps. When he stopped counting, I opened my eyes only to discover that he was standing in front of me with his nose an inch from mine.

"Is that face helping you?"

"What?" I asked, still panting and not daring to stop the exercise.

"That horrible, pained, ugly-ass face you're making. Is that helping you one bit? Is it making this any easier? Is it making the pain go away at all?"

"No."

"Then don't do it. It's wasting energy."

This was the first lesson in conserving and focusing energy that I learned from Jesse, but it was far from the last.

Within a week I found that I was eating healthier and more frequently, because I had to. I was burning energy at such a high rate, I had to eat better to keep from dying in there.

"You can control your body's metabolism," he said. "If you don't want to go through ups and downs, feeling full or hungry or like you want to take a nap in the afternoon, you have to eat five or six small, healthy meals a day. Your metabolism is like a fire. If you put too much wood on it, you'll burn hot, high, and quick, then die out. If you stoke the flame regularly with one or two small sticks, you get a constant, long burn."

I'd heard that before, so I knew he was right. But I'd had the luxury of ignoring that advice in the past. Now I was doing everything I could to keep my body up and running, because I knew what was waiting for me in the dojo.

One afternoon I finally asked Jesse why he kept the place so hot. "It's not hot in the winter," he said with a laugh. "I don't have any temperature control in here."

"Why not?"

He shrugged, then pointed to all the pictures on the wall and the trophies on the shelves. "All those guys whose asses I've kicked, they all work out in comfy air-conditioning."

It was as good an answer as any, and typical Jesse. He was never full of words, but the ones he used were usually right on the money. One day when I got there a little early, Jesse was standing in the doorway with a guy who had just arrived. "I'd like to test for my black belt," the man said. During the test, Jesse kicked the man in the gut so hard I thought it might have killed him. The poor guy flew backward and slid on the floor before hitting the wall. He grabbed his midsection and rolled over with a groan.

Jesse stood over him like a hunter over a wounded animal. "Are you injured or hurt?"

"What?" the guy managed to say. He'd heard the question, he just didn't get it.

"Are . . . you . . . injured . . . or . . . hurt?" Jesse said louder, as if the guy didn't speak English.

The man looked up and gave him a confused shake of the head. "What's the difference?"

"The difference is, if you're injured, I'll call an ambulance. If you're hurt, get your ass up."

After a second or two of catching his breath, the man got up.

Jesse had no patience for pseudo-toughness, and he would challenge anybody no matter what his size. I learned that lesson the hard way when I took my friend Ryan Mapston with me to the dojo. Ryan was an NFR bronc rider and a three-time Montana wrestling champion, a fact I made known to Jesse when he arrived. "So, you're a wrestler, huh? Big-time wrestler?"

Ryan didn't answer.

"You any good?" Jesse said.

"Not bad," Ryan answered.

"Want to wrestle me?"

Ryan didn't see me shaking my head and trying to wave him off. "Sure," he said. I just hung my head. Jesse pinned him in less than twenty seconds.

Jesse was also a stickler for technique. If I wasn't doing an exercise exactly the way he had designed it, he would stop and demonstrate, then make me do it again another hundred times until I got it right. Once when we were working on roundhouse kicks to strengthen the abductor muscles, my form frustrated him.

"No, no, no," he said. "Here, let me show you." He threw me a banana pad and told me to hold it and watch.

I knew what was coming so I braced myself for his kick as firmly as I could. When his foot hit the pad, it felt like I'd been kicked by a mule.

"That's the way I want you to do it," he said.

Every day he pushed me to the brink. I still had a life outside of the dojo—a ranch to run, business commitments to honor, and a social and family life to maintain—but if I ever had to chose between the workout and the other things in my life, the workout came first. That didn't always go over well at home. One night my girlfriend had planned a dinner party at the ranch with friends coming over for the five-course meal she had spent all day preparing. When I got home from the dojo, the guests were already there, but I couldn't even speak to them. I walked immediately to the rock floor in my living room, where I lay down in the hopes that the rocks would cool my body. I didn't speak to anyone and I didn't want anyone speaking to me. The dinner went on without me. Needless to say, things were a little tense around the house for a few days after that.

Jesse would just laugh at these stories, then put me through another grueling workout. He designed ab exercises that simulated bareback riding, and fast-twitch calisthenics to sharpen my reflexes for saddle bronc and bull riding.

"The abdominal muscles are your base," he would say. "They are your core. If you reach a point where they never tire, you have a platform you can build on." That is exactly what we did, working at least twenty to thirty minutes a day on nothing but the muscles from the base of my sternum to the top of my crotch. After six or seven months I reached a point where I could do ab exercises for hours without tiring. It would be nothing for me to drop to the floor and do a thousand crunches as a warm-up. It took a while, but I slowly began to realize how much Jesse had done for me, and how much more prepared I was for my 1998 return than I had been in previous years.

By the time I finished working with Jesse, I could stand flat-footed and kick the top of a seven-foot doorframe. I could do sit-ups for hours on end without breaking a sweat, and I could move in ways I hadn't been able to move in years. I was stronger, quicker, faster, sharper, more flexible, and had better endurance than I'd ever had in my life.

He had almost killed me in the process, but when 1998 rolled around, I had Jesse Marquez Lomalli to thank for my return to rodeoing.

9

Seven Times a Charm

CODY HAD RETIRED from riding by the time I came back in January of 1998. Like me, he had torn two knee ligaments while riding, but at age thirty-six and with a family and outside business interests keeping him busy, it was easy for Cody to call it quits. "I wasn't riding that well anyway," he said. "It was pretty easy for me to figure out that I wasn't coming back."

I hoped I could convince him to come out of retirement, not to ride, but to help me schedule my season. Cody had entered me and planned my schedule my entire career. If I wanted to mount a strong comeback, I needed my best friend's help.

"Hey, bitch," I said when I called him. "You getting fat and happy yet?"

"Not too fat to whip a little bastard like you. What are you doing?"

"I'm coming back. I was wondering if you'd schedule my year for me?"

There was silence on the other end, a long pause I didn't know how to interpret. Was he thinking about how to turn me down? Was he choked up because I'd asked for his help? Had he fallen asleep? Finally I said, "You there?"

"Shhh. I'm looking at the calendar."

Cody is a true friend, somebody I know I can count on to stick with me no matter what. People like that are hard to come by.

I expected my parents to be by my side. They'd loved me as a kid, as a world champion, as an injured man, and as a cowboy trying to mount a comeback. But I was really impressed by the support I received from people who weren't related to me: people like my sponsors, who could easily have turned their backs when I was down. Wrangler never flinched when I was injured. I kept them informed throughout every injury, every surgery, every rehab and recovery period, and they never wavered in their support. They were and are one of the best companies I've ever dealt with. My other sponsors, CLS Limousines and the MGM Grand, stuck by me as well. It would have been easy for any of those companies to move on after my first or second year-ending injury, and nobody would have questioned their judgment if they'd severed ties with me when I missed my third year in a row. But those sponsors told me they were with me for the long haul. It was a commitment I appreciated, and one I'll never forget.

I just hoped I could validate their decision with my performance in 1998. All those hours I'd sweated in the dojo, grinding it out with Jesse screaming at me, I never forgot why I was there. Any one of the three injuries I'd sustained could have ended my career. But I chose not to quit, not to let bad luck beat me. Whenever I wanted to slow down and catch my breath, I thought about what I was missing and how much I wanted to win again. Winning seven world titles had been my dream since I was old enough to have dreams. As long as I was able to climb over the chute, I was bound and determined to see that dream through to the end. Now, after working harder on my body than I had ever worked in my life, I was back. The big question was, how much of my old form would be back with me?

Cody and I mapped out a strategy to give me the best shot at recapturing the title I'd owned for six straight years. I would compete in fifty-six rodeos, the fewest I'd ever competed in as a professional and half the number a lot of cowboys would enter. But the fifty-six rodeos I would enter would be the ones with the biggest payouts. There was only one catch: I had to win.

I got off to a quick start, winning the Copenhagen Bull Riders Master Professional Series Finals in Denver, one of the biggest and richest events of the year. I felt a little rusty when I got on my first bull, but I rode him. The shoulder held up fine and my body responded well to all the training. I felt better, more toned, more alert, in more control, than I ever had in my life. Sure, I was only one ride into the season, but I knew all the effort had been worth it.

It didn't take long for me to get back in the groove. Roughstock riding is a little more complicated than riding a bicycle, but you never forget it. By the end of that first week in Denver, I felt great and thought I was riding better than I ever had before in my life. Not only was it like I had never been away, I felt like I was in better form than when I'd won my last title. I took second in the all-around that first week out, which I considered a great finish. I wouldn't normally be happy with a second, but after the three years I'd just gone through, I considered it a great start to a comeback year.

From there it was on to Fort Worth, Phoenix, Cheyenne, Calgary, San Francisco, the circuit I'd traveled my entire professional career. In every city the press wanted to know how I felt, and what it meant to be back. I would have loved to tell them, but I was a little gun-shy. During the previous three years, every time I'd said anything about how great it felt to be riding, I was in the hospital again before the ink was dry on my quote. Not that I was superstitious or anything, but I held my feelings close to the vest this time around. I figured I'd let the results speak for themselves.

They spoke volumes as the year progressed. Whenever I needed a great ride or a good showing, I was able to dig deep and come through. At the Houston Livestock Show and Rodeo, the richest rodeo of the season, I needed to ride my final bull on the final night to capture the $25,000 all-around bonus. Not only did I ride him, I scored 90 points, the highest score ever recorded in the Astrodome.

Later that year in Canada I needed to ride my final bull again to collect the $50,000 bonus in the Calgary Stampede, a bonus I'd blown a few years before when I let nerves get the best of me.

I drew a rank black bull called Black Jack that I scored 83 points on. When I made the ride and won the money, the crowd went wild as Tina Turner's song "The Best" blared over the speakers. It was a little over the top, but I'd be lying if I said it didn't feel great.

As the year went on and I became more comfortable talking to the media again, I made a point of thanking the fans and sponsors who had stuck with me through my injuries. I never let an interview go by without mentioning Jesse Marquez Lomalli and his Nippon Kenpo Dojo, and I always thanked my parents, Cody Lambert, Jim Sharp, and the rest of my friends who were there for me when things looked pretty bleak.

"I don't take my health for granted, and nobody should," I said on more than a few occasions. "When you're eighteen, you think injuries are for other guys. Now I know no one's invincible."

I'D NEVER BEEN one for slogans or sayings. I wasn't one of those guys who kept motivational quotes lying around or who bought books by coaches on how to win. But as my 1998 season rolled along, I remembered two old quotes I'd heard when I was a kid. The first was from Vince

Lombardi, who said, "Winning is a habit." The second was from Bear Bryant, who was a little saltier than Vince. Bear said, "Show me a good loser, and I'll show you a damn loser."

Both those quotes rumbled around in my head at various times throughout the year. Winning was a habit, a habit I had grown accustomed to, and one I wasn't too anxious to break. That led me to think about Bear's quote. I hated to lose about as bad as I hated anything. It didn't matter if it was a big-time rodeo or a game of backgammon with my dad; I would rather have taken a beating than lose.

Fortunately I didn't lose much in 1998. Perhaps the statistic I'm most proud of in my career was my win and place percentage during my comeback season. In the fifty-six rodeos I entered, I placed in the bull riding (the toughest and most unpredictable of the roughstock events) fifty-one times. That's a record nobody has touched. It also put me in the position I wanted to be in going into the final event of the year.

FROM MY FIRST week out through the end of October, I never lost the lead in the all-around standings. When the final regular-season event was over, I held a $40,000 lead and had qualified for the NFR in bull riding and saddle bronc riding. I'd been around long enough to know that no lead was safe, especially given how much money was up for grabs in Las Vegas, but I felt good about my chances. Given the choice of leading by forty grand or sitting in second place and chasing somebody else, I liked the view from up front.

It felt great to be back at the National Finals Rodeo as a competitor. Even riding into the arena during opening ceremonies was a thrill. For the first time I was selected to carry the Texas State flag into the arena on opening night. Though I had been the leading money winner from the state many times, I had never before carried the flag in because bareback riders didn't participate in the opening ceremonies. I didn't qualify in the NFR in bareback riding in 1998, so I got to lead the Texas delegation into the arena.

The sound of the crowd cheering as I rode past sent chills down my back like never before. This crowd knew what I'd been through. They understood the hard work and hardship I'd endured to be here. But they were also there to perhaps witness history. Through ten rounds this NFR would set an all-time attendance record of almost 175,000 spectators, all of whom knew that if I could put together a good two-week run, I would become the first cowboy in history to win seven all-around world titles.

I wasn't into all the storybook drama, although I realized it made great copy. I'd seen too many guys get too caught up in their own stories and forget about executing when the chute opened or the gun went off. The hardest event to win is the one you are supposed to. I'd seen that thousands of times in my career. The last thing I needed was to let the hoopla of my "miraculous comeback" distract me from the business at hand.

It had been ten years since I'd showed up in this arena as a college sophomore, a kid who didn't look a day older than fifteen. A lot had changed in those ten years. I'd gone from an upstart with a lot of potential to a favored world champion to an injured has-been. Now I was back as the cowboy everybody was chasing.

One of the things I loved most about my return to competition was the good times I had with other cowboys. We always kidded each other and supported each other when it was needed. A lot of the guys in the locker room had called and lent support to me when I was down, and I'd done the same for them. Now we were all getting ready for the most important two weeks of the year.

The locker room was a buzz of activity. As always, giant sheets of plastic were on the floor. The good folks at the Thomas and Mack Center didn't want dirt and tobacco juice staining their nice floor, so they taped down clear sheets of plastic that crunched when you walked on them. Tape and gauze littered the floor, and the lockers were overflowing with bull ropes, bareback riggings, and bronc saddles. Whoever designed the place had never imagined the lockers would be used for this purpose. If he had, he would have made them a hell of a lot bigger.

Because I hadn't qualified in bareback riding, I only had my bronc saddle and bull rope to worry about, which is what I was fiddling with on the floor when a bareback rider named Larry Sandvick walked in. Larry took his hat off and I burst out laughing. "What the hell happened to your hair?" I said.

Larry, who had never had much hair on his head anyway, had shaved his noggin as clean as a cue ball. With a little makeup he could have passed for Freddy Krueger.

"You kept telling me I didn't have any hair on my ass, so I might as well not have any on my head," Larry said. "My wife agreed, so she shaved it off this morning. This is the way it was when I met her."

"And she married you anyway," I said. Before leaving the locker room I couldn't help taking another dig at Larry: "Good luck, Chrome Dome."

I don't know if my ribbing inspired him or not, but Larry won the first round in the bareback riding with a score of 81 on a horse named Surefoot Sue.

I didn't do quite as well in my first go. I drew a saddle bronc named Wild Falls that I rode for 77 points, good enough for a three-way tie for fourth in the round, but not what I was looking for to get my week started.

Later that night I did a little better in the bull riding, scoring an 83 on Wedgehead. That was good enough for third in the round and an increase in my lead.

On the way back to the locker room that night, I stopped for a minute to speak to Tandy Freeman, who was, as always, the on-site physician for the NFR. When a photographer asked to get a picture of the two of us, I said, "Sure. Here's the guy who put Humpty-Dumpty back together again."

As I said that, I saw Chrome Dome Sanvick walk by, and it made me think. I hoped the Humpty-Dumpty thing didn't come back to haunt me.

• • •

WHILE I WAS putting together modest finishes in my first two rides, Herbert Theriot was placing fifth in the calf roping and splitting first in the bulldogging. I had done well, but he had done better. The margin of my lead was smaller after day one than it had been when we started.

The next day was more of the same. I got bucked off a bull named Henry, but rode a saddle bronc named Popeye for 79 points and a third-place finish. Herbert finished tenth in the calf roping and seventh in the bulldogging. Nothing to worry about. When they turned out the lights at the arena, I still had a comfortable lead.

That would certainly change in the rounds that followed.

In the next six rounds, I was bucked off three bulls and three saddle broncs, a terrible stretch for somebody who was trying to hold a lead. Getting bucked off in bull riding isn't that unusual. You can hit a stretch when the bulls are really rank and nobody rides them. That was the case in round three. Only two riders, Blu Bryant and Aaron Semas, stayed on their bulls that night. The other thirteen riders, myself included, hit the ground before the horn went off. In the fifth round only five out of fifteen riders stayed on their bulls. I wasn't one of them. Round six was a little better. Only nine of us got bucked off.

Of course, it worked both ways. In the eighth round only two riders stayed on their bulls. I was one of them, scoring an 84 on a bull called Rip Tide to earn second place. I also finished third in round four when only five riders stayed on, and I earned fifth-place money in round seven when six out of fifteen of us made it to the horn. Bull riding is that way. There are simply nights when the bulls win.

My saddle bronc results were a little more disappointing. In six previous trips to the NFR I had been bucked off my saddle broncs a grand total of ten times in sixty rides. Through eight rounds this year I'd been bucked off three saddle broncs, a terrible percentage given my history on bucking horses.

The horses were pretty rank, but that was no excuse. I just hit a midcompetition slump, one of those quarters where you don't throw a single completion or score a single basket from the floor. I had stayed on my horses in rounds three, five, and six, but the scores weren't much to write home about. Seventh place was the best I could muster in those three rounds. It was a piss-poor performance, and I have nobody to blame but myself.

What made it doubly aggravating was the way Herbert came on in those middle rounds. He finished fourth, second, sixth, and second in bulldogging in rounds three through six. He hadn't done quite as well in calf roping, but he had posted a time in every round. With two rounds to go, my lead had dwindled to just north of $35,000.

If I got bucked off my last two bulls and Herbert won a round or two, he would win, and I would go down in the history books as having blown one of the biggest comebacks in sports.

• • •

I DON'T NORMALLY read quotes or listen to commentary when I'm in the middle of a competition. It's distracting and counterproductive. There's nothing I can do about what others say. If I disagree with their comments, all I can do about it is go out and prove them wrong, and if I agree with them, I haven't gained anything. I always figured that the rides and the scores were the real story. If I took care of business in the arena, I'd either make the experts look brilliant or foolish depending on what they'd said.

I didn't mean to break that rule after the eighth round, but I didn't have much choice. "Did you hear what Harry Thompkins said about you?" a reporter asked after I'd finished my bull ride in the eighth round.

What a stupid question. I had just gotten off a bull. The only thing I'd heard was a buzzer. I thought about telling this reporter he needed to reevaluate the quality of his questions, but instead I said, "No, what did Harry say?" Harry had dominated bull riding in the fifties, so I thought he might have some encouraging insight into my performance.

"He said, 'Ty won't win it,'" the reporter said, reading from his notebook. "Then he said, 'In timed events they save the easiest animals from the previous rounds for the last two days. But in roughstock, they take the animals that have bucked everyone off. Ty will have to ride four really rank animals, and his chances of getting hurt are pretty high.' Do you have any comment?"

The comments I had were unprintable, so I chose to pass.

How could a former champion say something like that? Technically he was right: the timed-event guys were dealing with easier animals in the final two rounds than were the roughstock riders, but it had always been that way. Nobody had made comments like that in 1989 when my uncle Butch and I were battling it out for the all-around title.

And what was this about me getting hurt? Would Harry have said that if I hadn't spent the last three years nursing injuries? Why was I more likely to get hurt than any of the other cowboys riding bulls or saddle broncs?

These were all things I would have loved to say to the reporter, but instead I just said, "No, I'd rather not comment on that."

I gave more credence to Harry's prediction when I was bucked off a Kessler saddle bronc named Strawberry Wine in the ninth round. That was four saddle broncs I had failed to ride in nine rounds, my worst performance in seven NFR appearances.

Bull riding was a different story. As Harry predicted, I drew a rank bull called Sling Shot that had thrown Chad Brennan in the seventh round. But I was determined to ride that bull. When the chute opened, I kept it right in the center, even when he spun left the entire ride. When the horn went off, I stepped off and waved to the crowd. "This one's for you, Harry," I wanted to say. I scored an 83 on Sling Shot, which was good enough for third in the round.

When the dust settled that last Saturday night, I held a $35,467 lead over Herbert with one round to go. The math was simple. If I rode both my saddle bronc and my bull, I would win my second world bull riding title and my seventh all-around title. If I got bucked off both and Herbert won the round in either bulldogging or calf roping, he could beat me. It was the scenario I had dreamed about my whole life, and the one I'd played out a million times in my backyard on everything from a calf to a mechanical bull.

My destiny was in my hands. All I had to do was make the rides.

MOM WAS IN the stands for every round of this NFR, just as she had been every time I competed. My sisters were there too, but this time Dad couldn't make it. It was his busy time at the track, and he had to work.

The jockeys kept Dad posted, running out and shouting the results as they were announced on the television. I'm glad I couldn't see the expression on Dad's face that final day, because I'm sure he was a nervous wreck. Mom was as pensive as I had ever seen her, nervously shaking her leg and fidgeting as I prepared for my final two rides of this NFR.

Herbert continued his steady performance in calf roping. With a time of 7.7 seconds he finished third in the round and third in the average. It was a solid performance.

I drew a saddle bronc called Surprise Party, but it was

the horse that was in for a surprise. I'd had just about enough of my mediocrity in this event, so when the chute opened, I made the most technically perfect ride I could make. It was certainly the best saddle bronc ride I'd made all week.

When the scores went up, the crowd stood and cheered. I'd scored 81 points, good enough for second in the round.

I finished fifteenth in the NFR in saddle bronc riding, dead last among those who entered, but I earned $20,098. If Herbert or anybody else was going to beat me, he was going to have to put forth one hell of an effort.

I paid no attention to Herbert's bulldogging performance. It had no bearing on the outcome as far as I was concerned. I knew that if I rode my bull, I would win. My dad was a different story. Even though he was in New Mexico, he had his pen and pad out and had the scores and totals calculated to the penny. He knew what Herbert needed to do, and what I needed to do, and what would happen if the other riders around us did better or worse than we did. Just thinking about that stuff made my head hurt. But Dad loved it. It kept him in the game even when he couldn't be there.

Dad was outside on the track when one of the jockeys came rushing out. "Theriot broke the barrier!" he shouted. Dad dropped his head and let out a long, slow breath. Herbert hadn't given his steer an adequate head start (called breaking the barrier). He was penalized ten seconds. Even though he'd bulldogged his steer in 4.2 seconds (which would have been good enough for third place), he finished with a time of 14.2 seconds, well out of the running.

Dad knew before I did. I probably had it won no matter what. If I rode my bull, Hard Copy, there would be no question.

Mom stood up, then sat down, then stood up again.

Dad was starting a race when my turn came up. The jockeys called him over to the television. There was no way he'd miss this ride for anything. You could pick up the crowd noise on the telecast, or so I was told later. But all Dad was listening for was the horn. It seemed like an eternity for him, standing there with all the jockeys around him listening for any announcement.

When the horn in the arena went off, one of the guys next to Dad shouted, "He made it! He made it!" A hand was on Dad's shoulder and another was on his back. A third man grabbed his arm and shook his hand. But Dad just kept his head down and wiped the moisture from his cheek.

Mom showed no such reservations. She might not have been keeping score the way Dad was, but when I finished my ride and stepped off Hard Copy, she, along with everybody else in that arena, knew what I'd done. She and my sisters screamed and hugged and jumped like little girls.

I just stood there with my fists in the air, drinking in a moment no one had ever felt before. It had come down to one last ride. All the sweat, pain, doubt, frustration, and determination had all boiled down to this one moment.

It wasn't my style to stay in the arena, but I was going to enjoy this one for as long as I could.

• • •

LARRY MAHAN COULDN'T have been nicer when he met me behind the chutes. I don't know why I hadn't expected him to be there—everybody in rodeo made it to the NFR—but it had never occurred to me that he would be waiting for me when I finished.

"Congratulations, Ty," he said. "I've known for a lot of years that this night was coming. I'm just glad I could be here to see it."

"I don't know what to say, Larry. Thanks for being here."

"I wouldn't have missed it for the world," he said. "I had a good run, twenty-five years. Your name's gonna be on the top of the heap for a long time, probably longer than mine. Now you enjoy this time."

We'd both come a long way since that summer on his ranch in Colorado.

"Thanks for being here, Larry," I said. "It really means a lot to me."

Later that night, Larry told reporters, "I don't think anybody will ever beat Ty's record. As for me, my thing lasted for twenty-five years. If I'm concerned about that, I better check my ego."

It meant a lot to me to have Larry there that night. It was also special having Tandy Freeman there, and having my mom and sisters in the stands. Cody Lambert was at his ranch, but he was the first guy I called when I got back to the locker room.

"Hey," I said when Cody answered his phone. "You know what? There ain't but one son of a bitch in the world knows what it feels like to be a seven-time world champion, and that's me."

Dad couldn't be there in person, but he was with me every second of that last ride. He also knows more about the animals I drew, the rides I made, and the titles I won than anybody else on the planet, including me. Whenever I draw a blank on a fact or figure, I call Dad. Not only is he my biggest fan, he's a walking Ty Murray encyclopedia.

I don't know if Jesse Marquez Lomalli listened to or watched the NFR, but I know he was with me in spirit when I was grinding in those final two rounds. The last I heard from Jesse, he had sold the dojo and moved to California to become a police officer.

One story did filter back to me. As part of Jesse's cadet training at the police academy, he and the other recruits were sprayed with Mace so they would know what it felt like (and hopefully use good judgment before using it on a suspect). All the cadets were screaming, clawing their eyes, and falling to their knees. But when Jesse was sprayed, he stood stone still at attention. As his eyes swelled shut, he said, "Is that all you've got?"

I pity any perp that runs afoul of Jesse Marquez Lomalli.

10

The PBR

AFTER WINNING MY seventh all-around title, my focus changed a little. Rather than building my schedule around PRCA rodeos where I was competing in all three roughstock events, I began to spend more time at PBR events where I was strictly riding bulls. I loved bull riding and the PBR. Of course I might have been a little biased. I was one of the founding partners.

Like a lot of things, the Professional Bull Riders tour grew out of a series of casual conversations. In our case, the germ of an idea for the PBR started with a bunch of cowboys sitting around bitching about all the things wrong with rodeo and how much better the sport would be if cowboys were in charge. Everybody had an idea about how to make the sport better and more attractive to a mainstream audience, but it was the bull riders who decided to do something about it.

To begin with, bull riding is the most popular sport in

all of rodeo from a fan's perspective. It is the most exciting to watch in part because it's the most dangerous event. The wrecks are more spectacular and the threat of injury more severe than in calf roping, bulldogging, or even in the other roughstock events.

I've always likened it to downhill skiing. An expert can watch a moguls race or a slalom race and critique the skiers' form and technique, but when a guy who grew up in Miami tunes in, he's probably not very interested. Compare that with speed skiers, who are barreling down the mountain at over 120 miles an hour. Even the casual viewer tunes into that and is riveted. I don't believe fans tune in to see a crash (although some people do, just as some people watch auto racing just to see the pileups), but the element of danger draws people to the sport and makes them appreciate the athletes a little more.

The same is true for bull riding. There's a big element of danger in what we do. We average a wreck every seventeen rides. To put that into perspective, imagine if after every seventeenth play in a football game the stretcher had to be brought out for an injured player. That's what we deal with, and it's one of the reasons fans are so drawn to our sport.

Seventeen million Americans a year go to rodeos. Not all of them are cowboys and cowgirls, and a fair number are witnessing a rodeo for the first time. But they hang around until the end because they all want to see the bull riding. That's why rodeo organizers save bull riding until last. They know it's the most popular event, even among novice fans.

The bull riders know it too. That's why some of us decided to band together.

Part of the decision to form the PBR was financial. Bull riders knew they were the show at most rodeos, yet their compensation didn't reflect that. Rodeo purses had to be distributed among all events: calf roping, bulldogging, barrel racing, team roping, and the roughstock events. There was no other fair way to compensate all the cowboys. But it didn't take a Wharton Business School graduate to see the inequity when 90 percent of the people who paid admission to the rodeo were there to see the bull riding, but the bull riders were only competing for one-eighth of the total purse.

We might have been cowboys, but we could add. We knew bull riding was the biggest draw, and bull riders were subsidizing many of the other events. The question for us was simple: Why not give the fans what they wanted (more bull riding) and enrich the purse for those athletes?

Another part of our thinking dealt with the competitions themselves. Because there are so many rodeos in so many cities with so many cowboys competing, the bull riders found that the bulls weren't always the best, and the riders weren't the most talented. Plenty of times when I was getting ready to climb onto a bull I knew was a dud, I would look down the line and see some guy I'd never seen before getting on the best bull. That was deflating. I knew I couldn't score more than seventy points on my bull, and the guy who had the best bull in the herd couldn't have ridden a pony on a dude ranch. Too often on the rodeo circuit, the best bull riders and the best bulls were never matched up. This skewed the competition and injected too much of an element of luck.

We believed that if you could match up the best bull riders and the best bulls, everything would improve. The competition would be fairer and it would be better for the fans, which would mean it would be better for the sponsors. More fans meant more sponsors, which meant more money for the riders, which would lead to better riders.

That turned out to be the mission statement of the PBR: "The best riders and the best bulls for the best fan experience in the sport." The concept was simple, but sometimes the simplest things are the hardest to see.

In our case it took sixteen cowboys and a little common sense to create one of the most explosive upstart sporting franchises in the world.

WE BELIEVED THAT once you got that guy watching for two or three minutes of bull riding, he'd be hooked. Following it wasn't rocket science. You saw a guy stay on a bull for eight seconds, then a score went up. The guy with the best score won. It was pretty simple.

Because of the size and scope of the events, most modern rodeos had become more of a carnival than a competition for the spectators. For one thing, they lasted too long. The

Houston Livestock Show and Rodeo went on for ten days. A family might come out and watch a night or two, but few people hung around for the entire competition.

Even if you stuck around for the entire rodeo, you had to have a spreadsheet and a calculator to keep up with the scoring. Timed-event guys were competing against rough-stock riders for the all-around title. By the end of the third or fourth round you had more variables and possible outcomes than any normal fan could keep up with. I had more of a vested interest than anybody else, but I didn't have the time or patience to run through all the scores. It gave me a headache. If I couldn't keep up with it, how was the average fan supposed to?

We didn't have all the answers, and we didn't pretend to. But like a lot of athletes, we brought insiders' perspective to a sport we all cared about passionately. In putting together our ideas we decided that two nights of the best riders riding the best bulls would be ideal. We could have a round on Friday night and a round and a short go on Saturday night, put it on television, get sponsors involved, and see what happened. It was risky—nobody had ever challenged the norms of our sport before—but we were confident our concept would fly.

We also stole good ideas from other sports. The model we tried to copy was NASCAR, which had grown far more popular than the older and richer Formula One and Indy Car leagues. How had NASCAR done it? We didn't know all their secrets, but it was obvious to us that they had made their events followable and fan-friendly. They had opened up a huge new fan base by televising all their events; and they had built heroes out of their drivers. When you tuned into a NASCAR race, you knew what drivers were going to be there week in and week out.

We knew we needed to take a similar approach. To build a new fan base, we needed to build brand awareness around our riders. If we could keep the best riders in the public eye by putting them on television every week and allowing the public to see what kind of guys these bull riders really were, we could make heroes out of our cowboys and build a cult following for our sport. Everybody wants to be associated with a star. We just had to make our riders the stars of the competition.

The idea continued to take shape as more riders signed on and brought their perspectives to the table. We would need a cumulative points system that the fans as well as the rider could follow leading up to a world championship. We'd also need to establish a workable number of riders and make sure those riders agreed to compete in every event to ensure consistency throughout the year, again a model we stole from NASCAR. Golfers had a problem with having too many events that were too spread out, so Tiger Woods, Phil Mickelson, and Ernie Els were never going to play every week. That gave some events (the majors and a few others) more cache than events like the Texas Open or the Las Vegas Invitational. We couldn't afford to have a few guys show up one week and a few more show up the next. If we were going to do this thing, every rider had to be at every event. That was the first rule we jotted down on a napkin as we were outlining the bylaws of our new sports organization.

In 1993, sixteen cowboys and a businessman from Los Angeles named Sam Applebaum each put up $1,000 and formed the PBR. We elected a board of directors made up of Cody, Tuff, Michael Gaffney, Aaron Semas, and me. Between the five of us we had exactly zero years of experience on boards of any kind. We were cowboys. Some of us were ranchers, and a few of us had made good livings through outside business ventures, but there wasn't a lot of board-room culture in our group as evidenced by the number of spittoons we had around the table every time we met.

We began modestly with eight events in 1994, all tele-vised. Things went pretty well, and we built some brand awareness in that first year, but we knew we needed to take the sport to another level. To do that we needed a legitimate CEO, someone who could run the business day to day. "Who should we get?" Cody asked.

"Hell if I know," I said. "You know any CEOs that would work with a bunch like us?"

This went on for a few months. Then we ran across a guy who seemed perfect. It happened when Cody and Tuff were in California in the office of Randy Bernard, a Cal Polytech graduate who had worked in marketing at the Calgary Stampede and was now an entertainment promoter for the California Fair. Cody and I had known Randy from one of the promotions he had run at the California Fair, an event he had taken from a small-time local fair to a big-time enter-tainment and amusement extravaganza. Randy had paid Cody and I to come in for the fair and ride in a two-man bull-riding challenge match. At the time we were ranked one and two in the world. The event was a huge success and we liked what we saw in Randy. That led Tuff and Cody to his office to talk to him about promotions and sponsorships. We knew Randy was a creative thinker, and we thought he might have some good suggestions for promoting the PBR. During the meeting Tuff noticed a plane ticket to Colorado Springs sitting on the corner of Randy's desk.

"Why you going to The Springs?" Tuff asked.

Randy hemmed and hawed for a minute or two, then finally said, "To tell you the truth I've been approached by the PRCA about a job. I'm going out there to talk to them."

"What the hell you want to do that for?" Cody said.

"Well . . . I—" Randy started, but he didn't get a chance to finish.

"You need to come to work for us," Tuff said.

"You?" Randy was good and confused now. This was supposed to be a friendly chat about sponsorship promo-tions, not a job interview.

"Yeah," Cody said. "We've been looking for somebody to run the PBR operations. You need to come work for us. Be our CEO. What do you say?"

Before Tuff and Cody left Randy's office, he had signed on to be the new chief executive officer of the PBR.

Unfortunately, Tuff and Cody forgot to tell the rest of

us what they'd done. At our next board meeting in Las Vegas two days before the 1995 PBR World Finals, Randy walked into the MGM Grand boardroom and took a seat at the end of the table.

"What are you doing here?" Aaron Semas asked.

"I'm here for the meeting," Randy said.

"This is a PBR board meeting," Aaron said.

"I know." After an awkward second or two of silence, Randy said, "You don't know that I'm you're new CEO?"

"Our new what?"

Randy leaned over and put his head in his hands. He was off to a helluva start, but the fun was just beginning.

Later that same afternoon as the meeting was running a little longer than we'd hoped, Tuff and Cody got into a heated discussion over whether the purse at one of our events should be raised to $80,000 or $100,000. Cody wanted the extra twenty grand. Tuff thought eighty was enough.

"Save it for the Finals," Tuff said. "We've got limited resources and we need to make the Finals something really special."

"If we don't build these other events, there won't be any need for a Finals," Cody said. "We said we were going to do this thing right for the cowboys, and a hundred thousand is what's right."

"They're not going to bitch about eighty," Tuff countered.

"Well, you might not," Cody said. "But twenty thousand's a big deal to some guys."

"Look!" Tuff said, pointing his finger at Cody, but he never got to finish.

"Don't you point your damn finger at me, you son of a bitch!" Cody shouted, but nobody heard the words. We were all watching the chair Cody had picked up and hurled at Tuff's head.

It missed, but Randy, who was sitting next to Tuff, had to duck under the table to keep from being decapitated. The chair exploded into pieces against the back wall of the boardroom. "Come outside and let's finish this!" Cody yelled.

"I'm not going anywhere with you, you crazy bastard," Tuff said.

I'd seen these two behave like this before, so it was no big deal for me. They had grown up together, picking on each other since they were kids. Yelling and throwing things was nothing new. I knew that thirty minutes after the meeting they'd be having a beer together and making dinner plans. But Randy didn't know that. I could read his expression from across the room. He wondered what in the world he'd gotten himself into.

The meeting broke up without bloodshed, but that didn't mean Tuff would get out of the weekend unscathed.

Our sport got another boost of recognition later that weekend when Tuff, who was en route to winning the PBR championship title that year, went out for the final ride of the night on Bodacious, the two-time bucking bull of the year, and one of the rankest ones out there. Riders dreaded him. He'd thrown me twice. It was the perfect matchup for our grand finale. Plus it was nationally televised by TNN.

I figured Tuff would ride him. Bodacious had been ridden before, and Tuff was one of the guys who'd done it. I sure didn't expect the kind of wreck we televised to a national audience that night. Three seconds into the ride, Bodacious pulled one of his classic moves. He was notorious for jumping with his head back instead of down the way most bulls did it. This time he jumped and pulled Tuff forward. Tuff was leaning just far enough ahead that his face collided with Bodacious's huge head. In those situations the bull wins every time. Bodacious broke every bone in Tuff's face. It was the worst-looking wreck I'd seen in years.

I was concerned for Tuff, especially when I saw Tandy's expression when he got into the arena. They carted Tuff off with Cody and me in hot pursuit. Even if Tuff was okay, I wondered if this wouldn't put an end to his long and successful career.

My first guess had been correct. Tuff's jaw, cheek, nose, and skull were broken. He had a concussion and an injured neck as well. When we checked on him at the hospital that night, his head looked exactly like a pumpkin. He was stable, and according to Tandy, he would recover completely. As we were walking out of the hospital, Cody said, "God, I'm glad he didn't go outside with me the other night."

"Why's that, Cody?" Randy Bernard asked.

"Did you see him?" Cody said. "There's no way I could have knocked him out."

For the first time that night I doubled over with laughter.

• • •

I ENJOYED BEING involved in the business side of the
PBR. In the late nineties when it became apparent that we
were hitting the big time in the television market (by 1999 we
were TNN's highest-rated regularly scheduled program), we
knew we needed help. So Randy called in Barry Frank, former president of CBS Sports. Barry was the guy who'd convinced John Madden to get into broadcasting after hanging up
his coaching shoes, and also the guy who'd invented of the
Skins Game, American Gladiators, and *Stars on Ice.* When
he agreed to help us with our television rights, I knew our
fledgling little enterprise was on the way up.

But even with New York heavy hitters like Barry helping us, we were still cowboys who did things the cowboy
way. During another of our more intense board meetings,
we were negotiating a new contract with the MGM Grand
for prize money and profit sharing. We wanted 80 percent of
the profits. MGM wanted to give us 60. We wrangled and
cajoled them every way we knew how, but those casino guys
were master negotiators. They wouldn't budge.

Finally, after we realized we'd reached a dead end,
Cody said to the MGM Grand president, "Tell you what.
Why don't we cut the cards for it?"

"Yeah," I said. "Cut the cards for it. That'll settle it."

"Good idea," Aaron Semas said.

I thought Randy was going to fall over dead of a heart
attack. We were talking about a mid-six-figure difference,

but I realized we weren't getting anywhere by talking. The best we could do was take our chances with a deck of cards.

The casino guys loved it. They burst out laughing. Finally the president said, "I can't believe you want to cut cards for this deal in my casino. That's great!"

That's when Randy piped up, "Why don't we split the difference, seventy-thirty. That way nobody loses, and you don't have to find a deck of cards."

After another hearty round of laughter, we all shook hands and agreed.

I loved that side of the PBR, but I also still loved riding. I'd never won a PBR championship, and I set my sights on that after completing my seventh all-around title in 1998. I darned near got it in 1999. I won more money than anyone else on the PBR Bud Light Cup tour, taking home $395,725, and I won the World Championship Finals, which made me the reserve champion of the year. But I got edged out in points by a great kid named Cody Hart, who won six regular-season events and earned 10,100 points, 700 more than me.

I won the reserve championship again in 2000 and 2001, making over a million dollars in PBR events. During that time I hurt the shoulder of my free arm again, and I was consistently plagued by neck and hand trouble. My riding hand would swell up like a melon and become so sore I couldn't close it into a fist, and at times my neck hurt so badly I couldn't turn my head.

By the end of 2001 I was wondering what I was doing.

I'd made enough money to live comfortably for the rest of my life. I had a wonderful ranch in the greatest place on earth, with plenty of livestock and lots of things to keep me busy. I had been able to retire a half dozen world championship bucking horses on the ranch, where they could live out the remainder of their lives in comfort. I had a wonderful girlfriend. And I'd done perhaps the greatest thing in my life when I'd surprised my parents by asking them to move onto the ranch with me.

I'd picked out a spot near a small grove of trees on the opposite end of the property from my house, and during one of Mom and Dad's visits, we rode horses out to the spot, stood in the shade, and listened to the birds singing. "What do you think about moving here?" I asked.

"Moving to Stephenville?" Dad said.

"No. Moving here, right here where we're standing. I'd like for you to move right here. I can build you a nice house here in this stand of trees, and you can live on the ranch with me."

The next few minutes were pretty emotional.

What more did I have to do? It was a question I was asking myself more and more as 2001 rolled into 2002. What more did I need to accomplish? What other goal was I burning inside to reach? Then one night as I was listening to the wind rustle through the oak trees behind the house, the answer came to me.

And I was as calm and at peace with the world as I had ever been.

EPILOGUE

Hanging 'Em Up

BY MAY OF 2002 I was second in PBR points, and I was tired. On the thirteenth of May I picked up the phone and called Randy Bernard at the PBR office in Colorado Springs. "Hey, Ty," he said. "How's it going?"

"Pretty good. I've got some news for you. I think you better sit down."

"What is it?"

"Are you sitting?"

"I am now. What's up?"

"I'm retiring today. I've got a press release written up. I'll send it to you when we hang up." There was a long silence. Finally I said, "Randy?"

"Just a minute. I think I'm going to be sick." After another second or two of my hearing deep breaths, Randy finally said, "Look, why don't you ride the rest of the year. We'll do a farewell tour like Richard Petty did the year he retired. Every sponsor will promote it as your swan song. It'll be a big deal everywhere."

"You don't understand. I'm retired now, today. This is it. I've been thinking about it for a while, and that's what I want to do. I don't have the drive or the intensity I had before, so it's time to hang 'em up. I'm not interested in competing less than full bore. This isn't a sport you can go into halfhearted."

I heard a sigh of resignation on the other end of the line. "Okay, I understand. I'll put something together and get it up on the Web site as soon as your statement hits the press." Then he hesitated for a second. "You know what? I thought you were calling to tell me you were getting married. I went from a daily high to a lifetime low in two seconds."

We laughed and said our good-byes.

I needed to make a few other calls, but they could wait. Cody knew. He had suspected it for a few weeks, but I broke the news to him before I called Randy. I would call Jim a little later, then ride over to the other side of the ranch and tell Mom and Dad in person. I hadn't asked any of them for advice, even though this was arguably the biggest decision of my life so far. I'd always believed I would know when it was time to walk away from riding. When that time came, no amount of advice would make any difference.

My girlfriend, Jewel, had supported me when I told her down at the cabin about my decision. "If you're still passionate about it, if you still can't live without it, then you should certainly continue to ride," Jewel said. "But if you're just going through the motions, if you don't have that same fire, you should walk away. You've got your ranch, you're still young, you've got your health. What if you ended up paralyzed? You couldn't enjoy all these things you've worked so hard for." She was singing to the choir at that point. I had already made up my mind.

Of course Jewel was also right. I still loved riding, but I no longer had the deep drive it takes to be at the top of this game. That's the only reason I decided to walk away. My injuries had nothing to do with it. I was feeling good and riding great when I made my decision. But I'd accomplished everything I wanted in my career. Now I felt like I was on a treadmill, one season rolling into the next, each event looking too much like the last one. I still loved my sport, and I still wanted to be a part of it, but I knew it was time for me to walk away.

I sure wouldn't be bored. The ranch kept me busy, and I still had my obligations as a board member and founding partner of the PBR. I still had plenty of appearances booked and a little television commentating I enjoyed doing. Plus, Jewel had exposed me to her world, which was quite a different experience for a cowboy.

I've been fortunate in my life in that I knew what I wanted at an early age, and I never wavered. I'm not going to wake up when I'm forty and wonder what happened to all the dreams I'd had. I lived those dreams. I did the things I wanted to do, then walked away from the sport on my terms. It's up to others to determine where I stack up in the history of our sport or in the realm of sports in general. All I know is I don't have any regrets. I still have two-thirds of my life ahead of me, and I'm looking forward to living every day with the same passion and love for life that I had when I was a kid riding to Little Britches rodeos in the back of a Winnebago. People ask me what I'm going to do with myself since I'm not riding anymore. I tell them, "I'm not having any trouble. In fact, I'm barely finding enough time to just live my life."

Later that afternoon, after I'd called everybody I thought I needed to call and read through the draft of my retirement press release, I rode down to the breaking pen where Mom and Dad were working with some colts. "I've got something to tell y'all," I said. "I retired today."

"You what?" Dad said.

"I retired. I retired from riding today. I'm done."

Dad hadn't been retired quite a year, yet. He and Mom were just getting accustomed to that life, so I wondered what he would think about me joining him. He smiled, nodded, and said, "You little sumbitch, you couldn't stand to let me beat you at retiring either, could you?"

We all laughed. Then Dad said, "You know, I rode my last bull when I was the same age you are now. I hadn't planned it that way. But with work and you kids growing up, that's just how it played out. Pretty ironic, huh?"

"Yeah, I guess it is," I said. Then we rode back to their house and grilled steaks in the backyard, listening to the cicadas in the pasture as the sun slipped low behind the trees.

Pat Russell, the California rancher Jewel and I were camping with on September 11, once told me that being a great cowboy takes a lifetime of learning. As I've grown over the years, I've come to realize just how right he was. The true king of cowboys is part farmer, part veterinarian, part mechanic; a master horseman and a better-than-average weatherman; a skilled cowhand who can do anything with a rope; a businessman; and a conservationist who understands what it means to be a good steward of the land. The king of cowboys knows he doesn't know everything. He makes every day a learning experience. He also does everything in his power to carry on the rich heritage of the cowboy way, a way of life that has been around for centuries and will continue long after we're gone. Becoming the king of cowboys is like earning a lifetime Ph.D.

The cool thing is, I'm still a long way from being that guy.

Glossary

all-around. A competition for those cowboys competing in two or more events. The cowboy with the most cumulative points in two or more events either for a single rodeo or for the entire season wins the All-Around.

bareback bronc. A bucking horse rode with a handled rigging instead of a saddle.

breaking the barrier. A foul in bulldogging, calf roping, and team roping in which the cowboy does not give his calf or steer the prescribed head start out of the gate.

bull rope. A rope specifically designed for bull riding, with an adjustable loop on one end, a tail on the other, and a handle in the middle. The rope is pulled under the bull's belly and held in the cowboy's gloved hand during a ride.

bulldogging. Rodeo terminology for steer wrestling, a timed event in which the cowboy rides alongside a steer, then jumps from his horse and wrestles the steer to the ground. It was named after rodeo legend Bill Pickett, who is said to have become so angry at a steer that he latched on to the animal with his teeth like a bulldog.

car killed. A violent collision between a cowboy and the animal he is riding, resulting in serious injury to the cowboy.

changing leads. When a bull or bucking horse changes its lead foot, a sign that it is about to change direction.

chute. The cordoned rectangular area where bulls and bucking horses are held immediately prior to being ridden. It is in this area that the cowboy gets onto the back of the animal.

draw. The random pairing of animal and cowboy, performed by rodeo officials prior to the beginning of an event.

droppy. A bull that kicks during a jump while his front feet are still off the ground.

eliminator. An extraordinarily difficult bull to ride, one that "eliminates" most of the cowboys who draw him.

exposure. A prone position with your toes pointed outward during a bareback ride, a position that is technically and stylistically preferred.

hooked. Being head-butted by a bull.

NFR. The National Finals Rodeo, the season-ending grand finale pitting the top fifteen cowboys in each event together in a ten-round rodeo competition.

PBR. Professional Bull Riders, a relatively new sports league whose members include the top bull-riders in the world who compete in sanctioned events.

PRCA. The Professional Rodeo Cowboys Association, the oldest professional sports league for rodeo cowboys and the sanctioning body for over 700 rodeos annually.

pulled into the well. The centrifugal force formed by a spinning animal that pulls a cowboy into the imaginary circle at the center of the spin.

rank. A tough but good bucking animal; one on which a skilled cowboy can make a great score.

riding glove. The thick leather glove cowboys wear on the hand used to hold the rope, or rigging.

rigging. A leather, rawhide, and neoprene harness that is placed on the back slope of the horse's withers and acts as both a handle from which the cowboy holds on to the horse and a balancing reference during the ride.

roughstock events. Bull riding, bareback riding, and saddle bronc riding, the three judged events in rodeo.

saddle bronc. A bucking horse that is ridden while saddled.

snubbing. When a cowboy cradles a horse's nose in his arm and pulls the horse close to his body. From this position a horse can be blindfolded or otherwise subdued.

spur out. A required element in bareback riding during which the cowboy's spurs must be over the points of the horse's shoulders before the animal's front feet hit the ground the first jump out of the chute.

timed events. Events such as bulldogging, calf roping, team roping, and barrel racing, during which competitors are timed. The fastest time wins.

the well. The imaginary circle at the center of the centrifugal force created by a spinning animal.

wreck. A collision between a cowboy and the animal he is riding that may or may not result in injury; or the injurious throwing of a cowboy by a bucking animal.

Acknowledgments

THIS PROJECT WOULD have not have become a reality without the help and support of a strong group of friends and associates. A great thanks goes out to my publisher, Judith Curr, who believed in me and this project from the beginning, and to my agent, Tony Garritano, for shepherding this thing through. Thanks are also due to Luke Dempsey, my editor at Atria Books, who patiently weeded through the rough drafts and helped polish the words until they were perfect.

I also want to thank my good friends Cody Lambert, Jim Sharp, and Randy Bernard, who contributed in small and big ways to this book. Special thanks and love go out to my parents, Joy and Butch Murray, who made me what I am, and who made this book interesting and accurate. Their memories are a helluva lot better than mine. And thanks to Jewel, a real writer who read every word and who never wavered when it came to giving me an honest opinion, love, and support. Also Kendra Santos, who has loved and chronicled me since I was eighteen; all of her writings really helped this whole thing come together. Finally, thanks to my coauthor, Steve Eubanks, a true pro and new friend, who devoted a summer to learning the finer points of being a cowboy.